C000233177

RECENT DEVELOPMENTS IN RESEA
MANAGEMENT AT WORLD HERITAGE ᴗᵢᵢₑ

Edited by Melanie Pomeroy-Kellinger and Ian Scott

Contributions from

Dave Batchelor, Isabelle Bedu, Margaret Bunyard, Peter Fowler, Caroline Malone,

Katya Stroud, Tim Williams and Christopher Young

Illustrations prepared for publication by

Sophie Lamb

Oxford Archaeology

Occasional Paper No. 16

This book is part of a series of Occasional Papers published by Oxford Archaeology – which can be bought from all good bookshops and internet bookshops. For more information visit thehumanjourney.net

ISBN 978-0-904220-47-6

Typeset and printed in Europe by the Alden Group, Oxfordshire

Contents

List of Figures iv
List of Tables vi
Foreword *by Christopher Young* vii
Acknowledgements viii
List of Contributors ix

Introduction and Overview *by Melanie Pomeroy-Kellinger* 1

A Visit to the Maltese Megalithic Temples *by Katya Stroud* 3

Ħaġar Qim and Mnajdra Temples, Malta: a History of Conservation *by Katya Stroud* 9

Access and Visibility in Prehistoric Malta *by Caroline Malone* 15

Avebury World Heritage Site: Megaliths, Management Plans and Monitoring
by Melanie Pomeroy-Kellinger 27

Implementing a World Heritage Site Management Plan – an Outline of Recent
Projects at Stonehenge *by Isabelle Bedu* 33

The Stonehenge and Avebury World Heritage Site Education Project *by Margaret Bunyard* 43

Research Frameworks for UK World Heritage Sites *by Dave Batchelor* 51

Niuheliang, Liaoning Province, People's Republic of China: Strategies for the Management
of a Complex Cultural Landscape *by Tim Williams* 55

World Heritage, Landscapes and Politics: Some Thoughts from Current Work
by Peter Fowler 65

List of Figures

A Visit to the Maltese Megalithic Temples

Figure 1   Tarxien Temples: Excavations under the direction of Sir Themistocles Zammit, 1915–1919 5
Figure 2   Ħaġar Qim Temples 5
Figure 3   Mnajdra Temples 5
Figure 4   Ġgantija Temples: Part of the 3D digital model 6

Ħaġar Qim and Mnajdra Temples, Malta: a History of Conservation

Figure 1   Ħaġar Qim Temples: Drawing by Jean Houel, 1787 9
Figure 2   Ħaġar Qim: Lithograph of 1842 depicting what may be one of the earliest restoration
           interventions at the site 10
Figure 3   Ħaġar Qim: Plan published in 1886, indicating areas of excavation, restoration and
           proposed restoration works at the site 11
Figure 4   Ħaġar Qim: Restoration of the façade, interventions of 1910 and 1949–50 12

Access and Visibility in Prehistoric Malta

Figure 1   Tarxien: Plan showing features and locations of artefacts 17
Figure 2   Ġgantija: Plan showing features, and photographs showing views (a) inside and
           (b) outside 18
Figure 3   Tarxien: High and low visibility areas. Examples of images and vistas: (a) large bowl in
           SW temple; (b) view through SW temple; (c) large standing statue; (d) decorated altars
           and bowl on left side of SW temple; (e) libation trough; and (f) male animal frieze 20
Figure 4   Ġgantija: Plan showing levels of access 21
Figure 5   Brochtorff Circle megaliths 21
Figure 6   Brochtorff Circle: Composite picture showing reconstruction drawing, and (a) cache
           of semi-excavated figures, (b) figurine of carved seated figures (c) semi-aerial view
           of shrine megaliths 22
Figure 7   Brochtorff Circle: (a) plan of 'shrine' with stone bowl and bones and (b) photograph of
           the ochred 'cowrie' lady skeleton 24

Avebury World Heritage Site: Megaliths, Management Plans and Monitoring

Figure 1   Location of Avebury and Stonehenge in Wiltshire 28
Figure 2   Map of the Avebury WHS showing the location of the key monuments 29
Figure 3   Avebury Henge and Stone Circle: Aerial view looking North 30
Figure 4   Avebury: Visitor erosion along the top of the Henge bank 30
Figure 5   A buried sarsen in the lost Beckhampton Avenue under excavation in 2003 31

Implementing a World Heritage Site Management Plan – an Outline of Recent Projects at Stonehenge

Figure 1   Map of the Stonehenge World Heritage Site (2003 © English Heritage) 34
Figure 2   Stonehenge: Unparalleled in its architectural quality and as a feat of engineering
           (James O. Davies 2004 © English Heritage) 35
Figure 3   Stonehenge and its Avenue: a ceremonial route leading into the stone circle,
           and now cut by the A344 (NMR © English Heritage) 36
Figure 4   Normanton Down Barrows: since this area reverted to pasture in 2003, these prehistoric
           burial mounds are no longer isolated islands in a sea of crops (NMR 15041–06
           © English Heritage) 37
Figure 5   Stonehenge: sandwiched between the A303 and the A344 (Chris Newton
           © English Heritage) 40
Figure 6   Map of grass restoration in the Stonehenge World Heritage Site, showing arable
           areas that have been or will be reverted to grass between 2002 and 2012 (2005
           © English Heritage) 41

The Stonehenge and Avebury World Heritage Site Education Project

Figure 1   Examining the evidence 44
Figure 2   The children were keen to try the deerskin cloak of the 'Amesbury Archer' 45
Figure 3   Out of role children record their impressions of the Stonehenge landscape 46

Figure 4   The 'Tribes' barter their wares outside the stone circle at Avebury 47
Figure 5   Ceremonial dancing at Avebury 48

Niuheliang, Liaoning Province, People's Republic of China: Strategies for the Management of a Complex Cultural Landscape

Figure 1   'Boar' or 'Bear' mountain, viewed from the mounds at Location 5 56
Figure 2   The valley landscape of managed pine forest, terraced agriculture and low hill ridges,
            each of which is surmounted by a Neolithic monument 57
Figure 3   The outer kerb of Mound 4 at Location 2. This type of stone, perhaps micaceous,
            is particularly susceptible to freeze/thaw cycles, and has deteriorated very rapidly
            since exposure 58
Figure 4   One of the paths built under the World Bank programme. The path is hard wearing
            and clear, and built in a very different material to the monuments 59
Figure 5   The complex current landscape of archaeological features, in various stages of decay and
            excavation, modern agriculture, and tree planting, all set against dramatic
            topographic change 60
Figure 6   The current low level view makes the layout and scale of the monuments difficult for
            the visitor to understand 61
Figure 7   Location 2 seen from Location 3. Location 2 was a dramatic complex of monuments
            laid out along a slight terrace at the base of the hillside 62

World Heritage, Landscapes and Politics: Some Thoughts from Current Work

Figure 1   St Kilda: view eastwards from high above the west end of Village Bay, Hirta 67
Figure 2   Coctaca, part of the Quebrada de Humahuaca World Heritage site, Argentina 69
Figure 3   Tell es-Sultan, Palestine, better-known archaeologically simply as 'Jericho', is a
            large tell at the core of 'Old' or 'Ancient' Jericho as distinct from the larger modern
            town to the east 71
Figure 4   Mar Saba, Palestine, is an isolated, living monastery founded in the 5th century AD
            in El-Bariyah, the desert east of Bethlehem, where Jesus fasted and Bedouin still tend
            their flocks of goats 72
Figure 5   Ginkaku-ji temple garden, Kyoto, Japan 73
Figure 6   The Avebury landscape, Wiltshire, has motivated antiquarians and scholars, and inspired
            poets, writers and artists, here exemplified by the author's 'Avebury landscape 2', 2004 74

List of Tables

World Heritage, Landscapes and Politics: Some Thoughts from Current Work

Table 1   World Heritage Cultural Landscapes 2004–05: a Character Analysis......................................66

Foreword

Christopher Young

I am honoured to have been asked to write a Foreword for this volume of papers delivered in May 2005 at the Seminar on Recent Developments in Research and Management at World Heritage Sites. The Seminar was part of an EU funded project looking at World Heritage Sites in Malta and in Wiltshire in England. All the sites concerned are prehistoric and megalithic in character. The meeting naturally focused on them with some additional papers on more general topics such as cultural landscapes and research strategies and one paper on a Neolithic cultural landscape in China.

It might be thought that focusing primarily on two small groups of megalithic sites could lead to a narrowness of coverage in the seminar. Conversely it might seem that papers on more general topics as well as on a site from a different continent might sit uneasily with those devoted to Wiltshire and Malta. In fact this was far from the case and the papers as a group develop a number of common themes related to research and management as well as having a very wide range of coverage of different topics. These cover the history and character of the sites themselves, the use of modern digital techniques for analysing and understanding how the sites might have been used, the importance of understanding past conservation interventions, current management issues and management planning, the need for research strategies and the development of concepts of cultural landscapes. In doing so they demonstrate the endless fascination of our heritage, the infinite number of ways in which it can be studied and understood and its relevance for today and the future.

Nonetheless a number of common themes and conclusions emerge from this collection of papers. The first, of course, is the influence of the UNESCO World Heritage Convention. Far from perfect though it is, the Convention and its implementation have provided a framework for international co-operation for the protection of natural and cultural heritage. The Convention has also helped to develop a more uniform conception of the nature of heritage world-wide. Projects such as this one happened to a large extent because they involve World Heritage Sites. The Convention can be seen, too, however imperfectly, to be pushing towards improving standards of management and exchange of best practice. Much of the work described in this volume demonstrates the importance of international co-operation in this way.

The potential for international co-operation is demonstrated also by the involvement of the European Union AER Centurio Programme which funded the Wiltshire-Malta World Heritage Exchange Project. This relatively small amount of money enabled a productive programme of exchange of experience and of best practice between heritage bodies in the two countries. It is encouraging too that the EU was prepared to fund, here as elsewhere, work which promoted the objectives of the World Heritage Convention.

The papers demonstrate very clearly the importance of research not just to improve understanding but also as a basis for management of sites now and in the future. If we do not understand the nature and significance of the sites for which we care, how can we know what aspects need to be protected or enhanced or how these should be interpreted to visitors? It is also clear that research should address not just the archaeology of the sites but also how they have been managed in the past. The history of the clearance and subsequent conservation of the Malta temples discussed here, is vital to present understanding and to future conservation of the sites. This is equally true of the circles at Avebury and Stonehenge.

Equally important is the proper planned management of sites based on clear understanding of their significance. Fowler points out that many of the problems facing World Heritage Sites stem from the absence of management plans and of the consensus building and partnership which should underpin such plans. The descriptions of the Management Plans for Avebury and Stonehenge show what can be achieved even when very real differences of opinion among partners remain.

Less covered in this volume is the need to use the products of research and management of our World Heritage Sites to enhance understanding of them and to involve society as a whole in them. The Stonehenge and Avebury World Heritage Site education project shows very clearly what can be achieved for comparatively small investment in the educational field. Hopefully, it should have influenced the children who took part in it greatly for the future.

Taken as a whole, the papers demonstrate the strength of the concept of World Heritage and the ways in which it can be used to improve understanding and conservation of the world's heritage. They also show clearly part of the range of techniques and approaches which can be used for this as well as making very clear the integral link between research, understanding and management. Overall the volume and the seminar on which it is based contribute significantly towards the goals of international co-operation and exchange of best practice which are a key part of the World Heritage Convention.

Acknowledgements

Melanie Pomeroy-Kellinger wishes to thank to all the contributors to this volume and the seminar at the Institute of Archaeology, UCL on 25th May 2005. Particular thanks are due to Tim Williams and the Institute for hosting the seminar, to Professor May Cassar and Tim Schadla Hall for chairing the sessions. The Wiltshire-Malta Exchange Project was funded by Wiltshire County Council, English Heritage, Heritage Malta and the EU Centurio Fund. English Heritage kindly provided a publication grant to Oxford Archaeology where much help was provided by Ian Scott, Sophie Lamb, Paul Backhouse and Anne Dodd.

Katya Stroud would like to thank the following who, in their different ways, helped in making her papers possible: Isabelle Bedu, Melanie Pomeroy-Kellinger, Dr JoAnn Cassar, Dr Reuben Grima, Dr Nicholas Vella, Daniel Cilia and Anton Bugeja.

Margaret Bunyard would like to thank those most closely involved in the project and the organisations that supported them: Isabelle Bedu, Ros Cleal, Amanda Feather, Karen Hopwood, Gareth Owen, Melanie Pomeroy-Kellinger, National Trust volunteers and the staff and children of Amesbury, Preshute, Avebury and Kennet Valley Primary Schools.

Tim Williams acknowledges that his site visit would not have been possible without the support, time and enthusiasm of Professor Guo Dashun, Professor Wang Jing Chen, Professor Tian Likun and Professor Zhu Da of the Liaoning Provincial Institute of Archaeology. Their warm hospitality, both in Liaoning and at the Research centre at Niuheliang, was outstanding. The whole mission was only possible because of the tireless work and skill of Dr Qin Ling, from Peking University and the International Centre for Chinese Heritage and Archaeology. Thanks also to the International Centre for Chinese Heritage and Archaeology (http://www.ucl.ac.uk/archaeology/china-archaeology/index.htm) under whose auspices my visit to Niuheliang was organised. Prof Clifford Price, from the Institute of Archaeology, University College London, provided detailed advice regarding stone deterioration and conservation.

List of Contributors

David Batchelor, English Heritage
Isabelle Bedu, English Heritage
Margaret Bunyard, Wessex Archaeology
Professor Peter Fowler
Caroline Malone, Department of Archaeology, University of Cambridge
Melanie Pomeroy-Kellinger, Wiltshire County Council
Ian Scott, Oxford Archaeology
Katya Stroud, Heritage Malta
Tim Williams, Institute of Archaeology, University College London
Christopher Young, English Heritage

Introduction and Overview

Melanie Pomeroy-Kellinger

A seminar about recent developments in research and management at World Heritage Sites (WHS) was held on 25th May 2005 at the Institute of Archaeology, University College, London. The interesting and wide-ranging presentations were attended by an audience of around forty people in the Institute's seminar room. The seminar was part of a programme of activities contributing to the Wiltshire-Malta World Heritage Site Exchange Project funded by the European Union AER Centurio Programme with additional funding and support from English Heritage, Heritage Malta and Wiltshire County Council.

The exchange project was initiated by links identified between the management of Wiltshire's prehistoric World Heritage Sites (Stonehenge and Avebury) and those in Malta (the Maltese Megalithic Temples). The link between the Maltese Temples and 'druidic' temples in Wiltshire was made as early as 1886 by one of the first excavators of the Temples (see Stroud's second paper in this volume). The main outcome of the project was the exchange of professional experience between heritage staff via site visits, meetings, seminars and workshops. Key themes of the project were heritage management and sustainable tourism, heritage access and interpretation, management planning, developing research frameworks, and dealing with environmental problems.

The morning seminar session, introduced by Melanie Pomeroy-Kellinger and chaired by Professor May Cassar (UCL Centre for Sustainable Heritage), focused on recent World Heritage projects in Malta and Avebury in Wiltshire.

In the opening paper Katya Stroud (Heritage Malta) outlined the chronology and typology of the remarkable Maltese Temples, which date to the Neolithic period and are considered to be unique in the history of world architecture. The origin of this exceptional flourishing of monumental prehistoric architecture is still enigmatic. Less enigmatic are the serious challenges to the conservation and management of the fragile Temples caused by human and environmental factors. In her second paper, Katya Stroud gave a detailed account of the conservation of two of the best-known temples. The importance of understanding the history of the conservation of monuments and the long-term affect of the ways in which different generations have conserved and curated them were examined, and the importance of keeping detailed records of any interventions was stressed.

Continuing with the Maltese theme, Caroline Malone (University of Cambridge) explained how few places in the world offered such high potential for exploring issues relating to the visibility of and access to prehistoric monuments at the time they were in use. Using GIS studies at a site-orientated rather than landscape scale, Caroline Malone and her colleagues were able to explore how the temple structures were designed to work as buildings with their various levels of visibility and access. They were also able to study the placement of art objects in relation to the architecture at some of the temples. This exciting new research is able to suggest new avenues for the interpretation of how ritual operated within the Temples, bringing us nearer to an understanding of the function of these remarkable buildings.

Melanie Pomeroy-Kellinger (Wiltshire County Council) gave an introduction and overview to the Avebury World Heritage Site, exploring the repertoire of unique monuments and their landscape setting. The present management context of the World Heritage Site was explored and the development of the management plans and other management projects outlined in detail. An analysis of the strengths and weaknesses of the World Heritage Site was presented along with an assessment of the successes and failures of its management.

Dr Mark Gillings (University of Leicester) then delivered a stimulating and revealing paper on the implications of recent excavation work at Avebury and new interpretative approaches to Neolithic monuments and landscapes. (Unfortunately, the paper is not included in this volume.) Mark is one of the directors of a five-year excavation programme focused on monuments in the Avebury landscape where major new discoveries have been made. He started out by revealing just how shaky our understanding is of even this well-known monument complex, describing our knowledge as 'slippery' and outlining the many enigmas and puzzles relating to the monuments. Revealing some of the new sites discovered during his excavation project, he stressed the importance of conducting modern excavation in landscapes like Avebury and the key role excavation should play in development of research frameworks for such sites.

Indeed the importance of targeted excavation at World Heritage Sites has been highlighted even further recently by the revelations made in the summer of 2006 by Mike Parker Pearson and his team excavating in the Stonehenge World Heritage Site at Durrington Walls. Here, for the first time in mainland Britain, Neolithic houses have been discovered, probably representing a large village, contemporary with, and likely to be linked in some way to the building of Stonehenge.

Tim Schadla-Hall (Institute of Archaeology, UCL) chaired the afternoon session, which initially focused on developments and proposed plans for Stonehenge and recently-published research frameworks for World Heritage Sites. Taking a wider perspective, the last two papers of the day examined management issues in a Neolithic landscape in China and various cultural landscapes around the world.

The paper by Isabelle Bedu (English Heritage) emphasised that although Stonehenge is arguably the most famous prehistoric monument in the world, it is also one of the less well understood and less well presented to the public. The paper outlined the major changes proposed in the World Heritage Site management plan to improve the setting of Stonehenge, enhance the understanding of its landscape setting, and improve the conservation of its many prehistoric monuments. After describing the significance of Stonehenge and its surrounding monuments, it outlined the vision of the management plan, emphasising the importance of partnership and it provided an update on the projects underway to implement the vision.

One of these projects was outlined in detail by Margaret Bunyard (Wessex Archaeology). The Avebury and Stonehenge World Heritage Site Education Project was a pioneering scheme undertaken by a partnership of organisations in conjunction with a number of local schools in Wiltshire. Employing evidence-based classroom sessions, site field trips and role play, the project aimed to introduce a new generation of school children to their prehistoric heritage and to make the World Heritage designation of these sites meaningful to their local communities.

The importance of research at World Heritage Sites was emphasised again in the paper by Dave Bachelor (English Heritage) on the development of research frameworks for UK sites. Starting with an exploration of the origin and wider context of the development of research frameworks, it went on to outline the way in which UNESCO in various documents seeks to encourage their development. Using three case studies (Avebury, Stonehenge and Orkney), the paper concludes with an examination of how research frameworks can be developed and implemented, and can succeed in generating further interest and field investigation at these sites.

Having just returned from China, Tim Williams (Institute of Archaeology, UCL) enthusiastically outlined the outcome of his fieldwork in Liaoning Province. Niuheliang is an extensive cultural landscape with sixteen monument complexes, mainly dating to the Neolithic, and is on China's Tentative List. The importance of the visibility and intervisibility of the monuments is key to understanding the landscape here. The main excavated sites are deteriorating rapidly because of harsh weather conditions, and in his outline of key principles to underpin the area's management, Tim recommends the re-burial of these sites to ensure their long-term preservation.

In a very apt and exciting conclusion to the seminar, Professor Peter Fowler treated the audience to a presentation based on his personal experience with the assessment and management of World Heritage Cultural Landscapes. The paper outlines the characteristics of the 53 World Heritage Cultural Landscapes and the impact of the designation. It recommends that UNESCO's focus should now be on the identification and management of landscapes and the development of a philosophy and suite of procedures specifically for them. Derived from work and travels in this field between 2004 and 2007, Peter Fowler discussed his observations on a wide range of sites from the UK, Latin America, the Caribbean and Palestine. Outlining the wide range of management issues prevalent, the paper notes in particular that poverty and politics, religion and religious conflict are key management issue in many places.

One of the key themes emerging from the papers, and in the subsequent discussion, was that there are a number of effective positive management strategies which can be deployed to help mitigate the range of environmental and human factors affecting World Heritage Sites. The need to understand all past interventions and conservation measures taken at a site before proceeding with any major conservation work was evident particularly from the presentations on the Maltese megalith temples. The importance of research frameworks and an on-going programme of fieldwork and research (including excavation and new approaches to mapping such as GIS) were highlighted. A key message in most of the papers was that academic research fed straight into better site management through better understanding.

Almost all of the papers touched in some way on the importance of landscape and the difficulty of comprehending and interpreting landscapes, referred to by Peter Fowler as managing "poetry" in the landscape. The need for an integrated approach to landscape understanding and management was a main theme, as were the educational potential of world heritage sites, and the need for local community involvement in their management.

The seminar from which these papers have been derived was relatively low-key, organised at short-notice with limited publicity. However, it succeeded in attracting a diverse range of speakers and attendees, including heritage professionals from the public and private sectors, academics and students. This is testament to the growing interest in, and need for, specialist skills in the relatively recent field of world heritage site management. Indeed, there are already a number of specialist post-graduate courses in world heritage studies (in Ireland, Germany and Japan).

The Malta-Wiltshire World Heritage Site Exchange Project, which was the catalyst for the seminar, has really demonstrated the benefits of the opportunities for the exchange and sharing professional experience on an international level. Although all World Heritage Sites are individually significant and have unique values, the issues and challenges of their management, preservation and presentation are frequently similar, as demonstrated in the various papers presented below.

A Visit to the Maltese Megalithic Temples

Katya Stroud

The Maltese Megalithic Temples date to the Neolithic, from early in the Ġgantija phase (3600–3200 BC), to the end of the Tarxien phase (3150–2500 BC). These megalithic sites are considered to be unique in the history of world architecture on account of their well-developed architectural elements, superb artistic design, and sophisticated structural engineering.[1] At the time they were being built no other culture had produced such sophisticated free-standing structures. Since there is nothing remotely like these sites outside the Maltese Islands, their origin remains in question. Professor John D Evans (1959) was the first to look at other local evidence for clues about their origins. His theory, which is still the most widely upheld today, proposes that they may have evolved as above ground copies of the underground rock-cut tombs, like those found at Xemxija, dating to around 3600 BC. The similarity in plan is certainly suggestive and further support for the link between above ground Temple sites and underground burial chambers comes from the Ħal Saflieni Hypogeum, where certain parts of the underground structure emulate features found within the built monuments.

THE MEGALITHIC STRUCTURES

Architecturally, the Megalithic Temples of Malta share a number of common features. Each is approached across a forecourt, an oval space, which is overlooked by the building's façade. The façade is normally concave and is composed of a row of large stone slabs set on end (orthostats). The concave curve of the façade sometimes extends beyond the building itself, continuing as a free-standing wall enclosing a wider perimeter of the forecourt.

The orthostats support horizontal courses of smaller blocks forming the upper part of the façade. The centre of the façade is interrupted by a trilithon doorway. The doorway leads into an open space or court, with a semi-circular chamber, known as an apse, on either side. The court is usually paved while the apses have a *torba* (beaten-earth) floor. The chamber walls consist of two skins of masonry; an outer one constructed in large megaliths set alternately face-out and end-out in a header-and-stretcher technique and an inner wall constructed of smaller orthostats. The space between the two skins was filled with soil and rubble giving strength to the whole structure and tying the two walls together. The main difference between these buildings lies in the number of apses; some have three apses set on a trefoil plan whilst others have four, five or in one case, six apses.

Contemporary models and depictions of these buildings, as well as remains of corbelling resting on top of the inner walls, indicate that these structures were originally roofed. It appears that the corbelling was constructed of rectangular stone blocks forming a stepped dome. However, it is not clear whether the central spaces between the apses were also roofed or whether these were left open.

The prehistoric builders appear to have had a deep understanding of the quality of the rock used in the construction of the Maltese Temples. The building material used in these megalithic buildings consists of blocks of Coralline and/or Globigerina Limestone. Coralline Limestone is a more durable stone than Globigerina, but it is also hard to cut and shape. Globigerina Limestone, on the other hand, is very easy to carve and shape.

These rocks were often quarried in the vicinity of the Temple sites. Natural fissures found in Coralline Limestone enabled the insertion of wedges and levers to cut the rock into removable blocks. Globigerina Limestone on the other hand, splits less readily, but since it is much softer, more active cutting was possible.

Outer walls, which were exposed to the elements, were usually constructed in the more durable Coralline Limestone. Blocks along the outer walls were in fact usually roughly cut or split and left unfinished. Well-cut and finished Globigerina slabs were then used for internal walls. Assuming a roof covered them, these slabs did not have to be as durable as those along the outer walls, and by using this material a higher quality of finish could be attained in the interior of the building.

Artistic representations, in the form of architectural decoration within these sites, are largely confined to the first pair of apses and the court between them. These decorations mainly consist of patterns of drilled holes, known as pitted decoration, and stone reliefs depicting animals or spiral designs. Most Temples had structures within them that can be interpreted as altars and several sites have provision for fires, consisting of small reddened paved areas or low bowls. Additional interior fittings or decoration in organic materials have not survived, but their presence is demonstrated by the evidence of perforations in the doorjambs suggesting the use of wooden doors or leather screens.

Although these buildings have come to be internationally known as 'temples', we actually know

---

[1] Seven of the Maltese Temples are on the World Heritage List. The two temples at Ġgantija, Gozo, were nominated to the List in 1980. The WHS was extended in 1992 when five temples on mainland Malta were added to comprise the Maltse Megalithic Temples WHS.

3

very little about what went on inside them. The labour invested to construct these monuments is an indication of the importance attributed to these buildings by the community that built them. The nature of their contents excludes domestic or funerary use and they do not seem to be well-adapted for defensive purposes. On the other hand, structures, which can best be interpreted as altars, are quite common, as are the obese stone and clay cultic figurines found within them. The most obvious activity to have taken place within the Temples is perhaps animal sacrifice, evidenced by the amount of animal bones found within the structures and the numerous tethering holes present. Therefore, the primary use of these buildings seems to have been for ceremonial or ritual activity (see Malone, this volume).

Limitations imposed by the actual size of the internal spaces indicate that individuals or relatively small groups of people participated in the activities within. In some of the buildings small apertures, usually referred to as 'oracle holes', connect apses with inner chambers. Although this might not be the exact purpose that they served, they clearly provided communication between public and private areas of the building.

It has also been proposed that these buildings played an important economic role in the community, acting as redistribution centres for surplus produce (Bonanno 1986). The querns, stone mortars and hand-mills for grinding seeds as well as the large number of pottery vessels found within the Temples evidently support this idea.

A QUICK TOUR

The Ġgantija World Heritage Site was one of the first megalithic monuments to be excavated. The excavation, in the 1820s, was the initiative of John Otto Bayer, representative of the British Governor on Gozo. In 1827 Louis Mazzara produced the first description of the cleared monument together with illustrations. Additional excavations were then carried out sporadically up to 1954.

The Ġgantija Temples are found in Xagħra, Gozo and consist of two buildings constructed side by side and enclosed within a single massive boundary wall and opening onto a common forecourt. The South Temple at Ġgantija was built around 3600 BC, while the smaller building abutting it was constructed around 3200 BC. Both Temples have a neat unclut-tered plan of five apses in the southern Temple, and four apses and a niche in the later one.

The South Temple still retains both *torba* and stone-slabbed floors. Unique examples of prehistoric art, including altar blocks decorated with spirals in relief and pitted decoration, were found within the Ġgantija site. One of the most impressive features of the site are the walls which have survived to a height of just over 7 m in the façade and inner apses of the South Temple.

The site of Ta' Ħaġrat Temples in Mġarr, was first pointed out to Sir Themistocles Zammit, the Director of the Museum, in 1916. At that time it was a mound of soil and stones from which the tops of megalithic blocks could be seen protruding. The first excavations to clear the site of debris were undertaken in 1923 under the general direction of Zammit and continued until 1926.

Ta' Ħaġrat consists of two adjacent Temples. The older temple, dating to the Ġgantija phase, has a semi-circular façade with a monumental doorway, which leads into a rectangular central court. Three semi-circular rooms open off this court forming a trefoil plan. The second smaller temple is accessed through the eastern room of the larger building, which was modified in antiquity to make space for the second building. One of the most notable finds from this excavation is a small limestone model of a roofed Temple building, which is now exhibited at the National Museum of Archaeology in Valletta.

Close to Ta' Ħaġrat Temples is the site of Skorba Temples excavated by Dr David Trump in the 1960s. These excavations yielded finds dating from 5000 to 1500 BC, and provided fundamental information about Maltese prehistory. The earliest evidence for architecture in Malta, consisting of a wall belonging to the Ghar Dalam phase (5000–4300 BC), was excavated at the site. Remains of later shrines dating to the Red Skorba phase (4400–4100 BC) were also found, together with two megalithic buildings, which were constructed side by side in the Ġgantija phase. Later, in the Bronze Age, squatters made use of the Neolithic structures in the Tarxien Cemetery phase (2400–1500 BC).

Tarxien Temples is the most complex of the Maltese megalithic sites. It was discovered in 1913 when local farmers informed Sir Themistocles Zammit, who was then completing excavations at the Ħal Saflieni prehistoric burial site, that whenever they ploughed their field they struck large blocks of stone. At Zammit's request, the tenant dug a trench in his field, uncovering two large megaliths and a quantity of pottery sherds.

Zammit excavated the site between 1915 and 1919 (Fig. 1). It was the first prehistoric site where excavations were carried out stratigraphically and records kept of the progress of the excavation and the location of artefacts. One could say that this excavation marked the beginning of modern archaeology in Malta. Excavations started by exposing the South Temple of the Tarxien complex, excavating the cemetery inserted into the ruins in the early Bronze Age, then continuing successively to the Temple Period structures.

Further limited excavations were also conducted in various parts of the complex between 1921 and 1958. In 1997 the Museums Department conducted excavations in the areas just within the present entrance to the site and in the field to the north of the exposed remains. These excavations brought to light further megalithic elements indicating that

Figure 1 Tarxien Temples: Excavations under the direction of Sir Themistocles Zammit, 1915–1919.

Figure 2 Ħaġar Qim Temples.

the prehistoric complex extended considerably further than the currently visible remains.

The Tarxien complex consists of four principal megalithic structures. The small building at the eastern end of the site, which originally consisted of five apses, was the first to be built between 3600 and 3200 BC. The South and East Temples were then built in the Tarxien phase (ca. 3000–2500 BC), while the six-apsed Central Temple was the last to be constructed, towards the end of the same phase.

The South Temple is the most highly-decorated of all the extant megalithic buildings on the Islands, and contains a considerable number of examples of relief sculpture as well as the remains of a colossal statue. In a chamber within the thickness of the wall between the South and Central Temples are unique reliefs of two bulls and a sow with piglets.

The prehistoric sites of Ħaġar Qim and Mnajdra are found on the south-western coast of Malta, within the Islands' National Heritage Park, 2 km from the village of Qrendi. Standing at the top of a ridge, with the ground sloping down slightly on all sides, the Ħaġar Qim Temples must always have been a conspicuous landmark (Fig. 2). The island of Filfla dominates the seaward horizon here. The Mnajdra Temples, visible from Ħaġar Qim, are 500m away tucked into a small hollow above the southern cliffs. From Ħaġar Qim Temples the ground slopes gently downhill to the Temples of Mnajdra.

The prehistoric site of Ħaġar Qim consists of a group of three monumental megalithic buildings. It was first cleared in 1839 with further excavations in 1885 and 1910. Restoration works at the site in 1949 brought to light a cache of three headless statuettes and a fragment of a fourth, all depicting obese figures. It is clear that the main building at Ħaġar Qim was not planned at a single moment, but modified and extended over time, possibly in

response to changes and developments in the rituals and activities that took place within it.

The native stone found in the landscape has been employed in the construction of these megalithic buildings. In the vicinity of the Ħaġar Qim Temples, soft Globigerina Limestone is found and was used in their construction. On the other hand, at the Mnajdra Temples both Globigerina and the harder-wearing Coralline Limestone are found and both were used.

Mnajdra was first excavated in 1840, a year after Ħaġar Qim, and was then investigated further through various excavations carried out at the site throughout the 20th century. Remarkable finds uncovered during these excavations include examples of clay vessels decorated with various intricate designs, flint tools, as well as a clay representation of a human head.

Mnajdra consists of three separate buildings overlooking a common forecourt (Fig. 3). The first and oldest structure is the small Upper Temple built some time between 3600 and 3200 BC. The Lower Temple with its concave façade was next to be built at the beginning of the Tarxien phase, around 3150 BC, followed by the Central Temple which was

Figure 3 Mnajdra Temples.

constructed on an artificial platform between the two earlier buildings.

The Lower building at Mnajdra is exceptional in that it was built so that it marked the four seasons. During the Spring and Autumn Equinoxes the sun rises in the centre of its main doorway, while during the Summer and Winter Solstices the beams of the rising sun pass along the sides of the main doorway hitting two decorated slabs within the first chambers.

MEETING OUR CHALLENGES

Managing and preserving these sites is an immense challenge both because of the monuments' intrinsic nature, and because of the increasing demands being made on them by various sections of modern society.

The materials used in the construction of these buildings as well as their structural properties, combined with the climate and environment of the Maltese Islands have presented us with particular problems of deterioration and dictate the manner in which we have to approach the preservation of these sites. Surface powdering and flaking of the stone is particularly manifest in Globigerina Limestone. Its main cause is a combination of the intrinsic properties of the stone, such as its high porosity, combined with external conditions, such as rain, marine aerosol, ground salts, temperature fluctuations, and strong winds, which in turn are dictated by the monument's location and architectural form.

The most obvious structural change that the megalithic structures have undergone since their original construction is the loss of their roofing system. This has left areas of the buildings, which were presumably sheltered, exposed to the elements. One of the most significant structural consequences of this is the effect of rain on the infill between the inner and outer masonry skins, which on occasion, has led to the collapse of sections of the monuments.

Saturation of the soil infill by rainwater has resulted in the leaching out of the soil through the vertical joints between the stone uprights. The soil originally placed between the two skins of masonry served to add weight to the inner wall, and hence increase its stability. If the soil is leached out, or if the outward pressure of the soil (and the water it contains) exceeds the inner thrust of the blocks, then the latter can easily collapse.

Human activity including quarrying, vandalism and even tourism further compound the problems of structural stability. In the past vibrations from quarrying operations were detrimental, with each input of dynamic energy contributing to the propagation of micro-fissures and possibly even to the destabilisation of blocks.

The lack of visitor-flow management in the past may also have contributed to the decay of the sites.

Figure 4 Ġgantija Temples: Part of the 3D digital model.

For a long time visitors were allowed to roam the sites freely, with the result that they walked on the walls and the megaliths endangering their stability. Wear and tear on the Temples' floors by visitors has also encouraged water ponding within the apses, which further contributes to the deterioration of these monuments.

These are the challenges that Heritage Malta[2] has chosen to tackle since its inception in 2002. It has launched a number of projects for the better management and preservation of the Megalithic Temples. Plans are well underway for the construction of three on-site visitor centres; one at Ħagar Qim, another at Tarxien and a third at Ġgantija. These centres will offer on-site interpretation facilities, which until now have not been possible, because of the nature of the sites.

Other extensive projects launched in 2004 and 2005 involve the environmental monitoring of two of these sites. Here the latest technology is being utilised to monitor and record rainfall, air temperature, humidity, wind speed and direction, changes in the megaliths' temperatures, water flow through the site, and soil erosion; all parameters which are indicative of potential deterioration in the Megalithic Temples. In addition, detailed documentation in the form of three-dimensional digital models of the sites is being carried out for each of the monuments (Fig. 4).

This is the first time in the history of the Megalithic Temples of Malta that such extensive projects have been undertaken for their management and preservation, marking an important milestone in ensuring a future for these sites.

---

[2] Heritage Malta is the national agency of the Government for Malta, set up in 2002 and entrusted with the conservation and management of the national museums, heritage sites and collections.

Bibliography

Bonanno, A, 1986 A Socio-economic Approach to Maltese Prehistory, *Malta: Studies of its Heritage and History*, Valletta, 17–46

Evans, J D, 1953 The Prehistoric Culture Sequence in the Maltese Archipelago, *Proc Prehist Soc* **2**, 41–94

Evans, J D, 1959 *Malta*, London

Evans, J D, 1971 *The Prehistoric Antiquities of the Maltese Islands: A Survey*, London

Trump, D H, 1966 *Skorba: Excavations carried out on behalf of the National Museum of Malta, 1961–63.*

Reports of the Research Committee of the Society of Antiquaries of London, **22**, London & National Museum of Malta

Trump, D H, 2002 *Malta: Prehistory and Temples*, Malta

Zammit, T, 1927 *The Neolithic Temples of Hajar Kim and Mnaidra and the "Miska" Reservoirs*, Valletta

Zammit, T, 1930 The Prehistoric Remains of the Maltese Islands, *Antiquity* **4** (**13**), 55–79

Ħaġar Qim and Mnajdra Temples, Malta: a History of Conservation

Katya Stroud

Each generation of archaeologists, curators, conservators and restorers has left their mark on the Maltese Megalithic Temples. The prehistoric monuments that we see today consist of the original prehistoric structures as well as the various elements that were introduced to them as part of past conservation and restoration interventions. The cracked block that was repaired, the megalith that was lifted, the wall that was rebuilt; all have contributed to the reshaping of the archaeological record that we have inherited of the Prehistoric Temples on the Islands of Malta and Gozo.

Therefore, in trying to understand these sites, one has to take into consideration that their story did not end in the past, with their abandonment in prehistory or their eventual burial; they underwent drastic changes even after they were brought to light by their excavators, and in some cases are still undergoing change today. Therefore, it is not only our perception and understanding of the past that is changing, but it is also the actual physical archaeological record that is dynamic because of the way we approach, curate and preserve it.

FIRST REFERENCES

Ħaġar Qim Temples were first mentioned in literature in 1647 in *Della Descrittione di Malta* by Giovanni Francesco Abela, member of the Order of the Knights of St John. In this factual description of various aspects of the Maltese Islands and its inhabitants, Abela mentions the Megalithic Temples and describes them as being the remains of buildings constructed by giants, whom he assumes had inhabited the Maltese Islands in the past.

The first graphic depiction of Ħaġar Qim, on the other hand, dates to the 1780s. During his travels around Sicily, Lipari and Malta, Jean Houel, engraver to King Louis XVI of France, painted numerous pictures of ancient buildings that he visited. Each drawing was accompanied by a short description and these were later published as *Voyage Pittoresque des isles de Sicile, de Lipari, et de Malte* in 1787. One of the published pictures shows the remains of the main building at Ħaġar Qim and the accompanying description says that the building originally had a circular ground plan and was built in large blocks of stone (Fig. 1). This drawing shows that the majority of the site was buried at the time but that the main larger megaliths were visible protruding from the soil.

In 1804 Louis de Boisgelin added to Houel's description saying that the foundations of the walls

Figure 1　Ħaġar Qim Temples: Drawing by Jean Houel, 1787.

of this circular structure could be traced, 'running in lines across the extent of this vast enclosure'. Boisgelin also provides the first theory for the original use of the remains since he suggests that they may be the remains of houses.

It was Onorato Bres, in 1816, who first ascribed the remains of Ħaġar Qim to the Phoenicians; an attribution that would last almost a century. In his *Malta Antica Illustrata*, Bres uses a different approach to the understanding of these prehistoric monuments, dismissing Abela's 'giant' theory as a *favola* (fairy-tale) saying that it is more probable that they were built by the Phoenicians.

The first to refer to the remains as being those of 'temples' was Albert de La Marmora, a French archaeologist who visited the Maltese Islands in 1834. In 1836 he published a report about Ġgantija Temples in Gozo: *Lettre a Monsieur Raoul Rochette, Membre de l'Institut Archéologique, sur le Temple de L-Ile de Gozo, dit La Tour Des Géants*. In this letter, La Marmora refers to Ħaġar Qim, describing it as a temple with an outer *temenos*. It seems that earlier authors had neglected to mention this *temenos*, or possibly it may have been a modern addition to the remains, which La Marmora took to be original.

1839–40 EXCAVATIONS

The visible megaliths seem to have attracted relatively early curiosity about the site and this is probably how it came to be excavated as early as 1839. Ħaġar Qim was in fact the second Temple site to be excavated on the Maltese Islands, the first being Ġgantija Temples which were cleared in the 1820s.

9

Funds for the excavation had been set aside by the then Governor of Malta Sir Henry Bouverie. J G Vance, an officer of the Royal Engineers, undertook the supervision of the excavation which started in November and lasted three months. On completion of the excavation, Lt W Foulis drew up a plan of the site, however, the only record of these excavations is a short description published in the *Malta Times* in 1840 and a slightly more detailed account of the finds with some views of the remains by Basire, published in *Archaeologia* in 1842.

These accounts give a detailed description of the remains that were uncovered, but do not provide much information on the excavations themselves. It is most likely that the 'excavation' took the form of a clearance exercise, and that soil and rubble were removed from the site with the aim of uncovering the remains of the building. Vance (1842) does record a number of observations he made during the course of this exercise, mentioning that the remains of the main building seem to be split into a northern and southern division and that 'nearly all the walls on the northern division bear evident marks of the action of fire, some of them, indeed, being quite rotten and having the red appearance of bricks'. A total of nine statuettes were collected from the remains; seven of these figures were worked in stone and depicted a seated obese figure. In addition, fragments of pottery, including bowls, small jugs and lamps, a stone slab decorated with spirals, and three altars were found.

The first restoration work on the site may have been carried out during or just after these first excavations. A lithograph of one of the chambers published in 1842 depicts stone pillars supporting three broken horizontal slabs (Fig. 2). Judging by this drawing, as well as a photograph of the same features published in 1901, these pillars seem to be modern since they are built of small worked ashlar blocks and were most probably inserted to support the broken slabs at the time of their discovery or shortly afterwards.

Figure 2 Ħaġar Qim: Lithograph of 1842 depicting what may be one of the earliest restoration interventions at the site.

Although the insertion of these supports appears to be an intrusive intervention, it is easy to identify as a modern addition. It is also completely reversible once a suitable alternative is found and does not have an adverse effect on the remains since it utilises the same materials as the original. In other words, this crude intervention aimed at preserving some original features of the site and carried out around 1839–40, would have met today's international standards for the preservation of historical monuments.

NEW THEORIES AND EXCAVATIONS

Although the excavation of the site was not well-documented, the uncovering of new features gave rise to numerous new theories regarding the megalithic structures and their origins. In 1870 Professor Andrew Leith Adams put forward a new theory in *Notes of a Naturalist in the Nile Valley and Malta*, suggesting that they were close to, or formed part of, an important sea-port town. At this time these monuments were still believed to be of Phoenician origin, and in 1872 Dr Cesare Vassallo not only attributed the Ħaġar Qim to the Phoenicians, but also gives 1400 BC as the date for the beginning of the Phoenician period in Malta.

In June 1885 a proposal was made to build a rubble wall around Ħaġar Qim, but as the remains had never been thoroughly surveyed and their extent never actually ascertained, it was decided to carry out excavation works before the erection of such a wall. Following orders given by the Governor Sir John Lintorn Arabin Simmons, Dr A A Caruana, Librarian to the Government Public Library, who was also in charge of the museum of the Public Library at the time, made some supplementary excavations at the site between the August and December of 1885.

An extensive restoration programme was also launched at the time by Dr Caruana, with the view that 'some of these imposing works of Cyclopean art might be made, with a little skilful restoration, to look almost as complete as when they were originally constructed' (1886). However, this aim of making the site look as close as possible to its original appearance was not completely implemented.

Drawings of the remains by Vassallo were published in Caruana's report in 1886. The colour-coding on the plan he produced shows the areas that were excavated at the time, areas that were restored and other parts of the monument for which Caruana suggested restoration, but which were not restored at the time (Fig. 3).

The plan in fact shows that a number of collapsed megaliths were replaced in their original positions, whilst others were repaired. Elevation drawings also produced by Vassallo indicate that a wall at the rear of an external niche at Ħaġar Qim was reconstructed in small rubble.

The possibility that the remains actually pre-dated the Phoenician period was taken into consideration for the first time in Caruana's report of 1886. In his

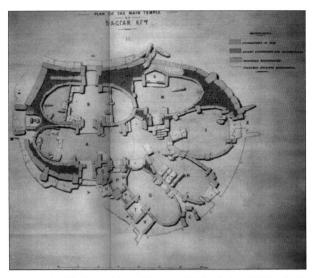

Figure 3 Ħaġar Qim: Plan published in 1886, indicating areas of excavation, restoration and proposed restoration works at the site.

publication Caruana compares the structures to 'druidical temples found abroad' and suggests that the possibility of an earlier date for the remains at Ħaġar Qim should be investigated.

1910 EXCAVATIONS

Caruana's proposals for future restoration were in a large part implemented in 1910. At this time, further excavations, as well as extensive restoration works, were carried out at Ħaġar Qim by the British School at Rome under the direction of Dr Thomas Ashby, and in collaboration with Sir Themistocles Zammit then Director of the Museum. These excavations were the first to be conducted in a scientific manner at this site and for which records were kept of the progress of the excavation and of the stratigraphy uncovered (Ashby *et al.* 1913).

The restoration works which accompanied the renewed excavations included the replacement of the modern supporting pillars inserted in 1839 as well as major restoration works on the main building's façade. Large blocks lying on the ground in front of the entrance were lifted to form part of the top horizontal courses of the façade. The lintel was repaired but left on the ground in front of the main entrance.

It was also during this wave of restoration interventions that a considerable amount of Portland cement was used in repairing cracked or broken megaliths. Nowadays it is a well-known fact that this material introduces harmful salts to limestone. Nevertheless, at the time, no adequate alternative material was available for the repair of broken megaliths. Cement was the material of choice for restoration and reconstruction in the first half of the 20th century and it was commonly used at other major archaeological sites during this period, such as

at Knossos. The use of concrete for the consolidation of ancient monuments had even been commended in 1931 when the *Athens Charter for the Restoration of Historic Monuments* encouraged the use of modern materials in the restoration of historic buildings.

It is evident that restoration of any megaliths was based on a sensible judgement of all the available evidence to identify their original location (anastylosis). It also appears that no work was carried out in areas where there was doubt as to the original position of the building's dislodged structural elements.

TEMPLE ROOFING

With this new scientific approach to the discovery and understanding of these prehistoric buildings, studies seem to take a different direction, with an increasing interest in the structural aspects of these monuments.

In 1932, Professor T Eric Peet, who had participated in the excavation of Ħaġar Qim with Ashby and Zammit, presented the idea that the Temples were originally covered, proposing that the apsed chambers were originally roofed with corbelling, whilst the central areas were likely to have been left uncovered (Peet 1932).

The question of roofing was again addressed in 1934 by Professor Luigi M. Ugolini in *Malta; origini della civilta mediterranea*, where he maintains that the prehistoric monuments were completely roofed over by a stone vault. This theory was further supported by Architect Carlo Ceschi who published his study on the architecture of these buildings – *Architettura dei templi megalitici di Malta* – in 1939.

POST-WORLD WAR II RESTORATION

In the late 1940s and early 1950s large-scale restoration works were carried out at the site under the direction of Dr Baldacchino, then Director of the Museums Department. At this time, the approach used for the post-war rebuilding and restoration of historic and modern buildings in the war-torn villages of Malta and in the city of Valletta may have influenced the methods adopted in the restoration of this prehistoric monument.

It was during this phase of restoration works that the façade of Ħaġar Qim saw the most drastic changes. During the spring of 1949, the lintel, which had been repaired in 1910, was reinstated within the façade, capping the entrance to the main building. Unfortunately, by 1958 this lintel developed a longitudinal crack and had to be repaired once more, this time by means of bronze cleats and rods.

As part of the 1949 intervention, two courses of masonry overlying the façade's orthostats were also rebuilt (Fig. 4). The origin of the stone blocks forming these courses is not clear, although some may have been retrieved during the clearance of soil that lay against the lower parts of the façade itself. However, given the lack of evidence available for the original location of the dislodged megaliths, it is likely that

Legend:
Restoration/Anastylosis in 1910
Restoration/Anastylosis in 1948-49
Encasing in cement in 1949

Figure 4 Ħaġar Qim: Restoration of the façade, interventions of 1910 and 1949–50.

the restoration was influenced by the restorers' impressions of what the original façade could have looked like, rather than by any attempts to discover the original location of displaced elements.

Later in 1949, some of the broken megaliths forming part of the façade were reconstructed using cement mixed with Globigerina chippings. A number of megaliths found within the main building, which had deteriorated considerably were also replaced by modern blocks. However, there is nothing on site, and no records exist, to indicate which blocks were actually replaced. It is therefore impossible today to identify which blocks were inserted in 1949.

SETTLING A LONG DEBATE

By this time, the debate regarding the age of the prehistoric monuments on the Islands had still not been settled. A grant from the Inter-University Council for Higher Education in the Colonies to the Royal University of Malta gave the opportunity for a detailed re-examination of the prehistoric evidence for the Maltese Islands. In 1952 Professor John D Evans was given the responsibility of co-ordinating this new survey of all the prehistoric monuments. Through cross-dating the typological sequence of local pottery with the Sicilian sequence, Evans was able to create a chronology for Maltese prehistory, which was published in *Proceedings of the Prehistoric Society* in 1953.

In the spring of 1954 a number of trenches were excavated within Ħaġar Qim with the objective of correlating the remains with the newly-established sequence. However, it was not until Dr David Trump's excavation of Skorba, between 1961 and 1963, as well as the eventual calibration of the radiocarbon dates obtained from these excavations, that Ħaġar Qim could be dated to around 3600 BC.

RECENT INTERVENTIONS

Further minor restoration work at Ħaġar Qim was carried out in the 1980s. In 1990 Arch. Gennaro Tampone and the team participating in the Malta-Florence bilateral project, lifted a number of upright blocks which were in danger of collapsing and placed them back in their original position, inserting lead wedges underneath them to make them more stable. These blocks still appear to be structurally stable although the lead wedges have become quite misshapen due to the pressure exerted on them by the overlying stone blocks.

The most extensive recent works at Ħaġar Qim involved the restoration of a wall that collapsed following a severe rainstorm in November 1998. Restoration included a detailed study of the manner in which the collapse occurred, a study of photographs of the site prior to the collapse, and the replacement of dislodged megaliths in their original positions. A pillar constructed out of modern Globigerina blocks had to be inserted in the place of a megalith that had completely disintegrated, but otherwise all the megaliths were replaced in their original locations.

CONCLUSIONS

One general problem in tracing a site's history is the lack of records kept of restoration and conservation interventions making it difficult to identify what is original and what has been restored, and also making it difficult to determine how true to the original any restoration work was. Luckily we do have graphic records for the site, such as paintings and photographs which are invaluable in identifying restoration interventions and their extent. Nonetheless, it has become apparent that a study of the more recent history of the prehistoric Temples is essential in understanding the most substantial material evidence for our prehistory – the prehistoric monuments themselves.

On the other hand, the transformation of these monuments in their recent history should also be taken as an opportunity. Through it, the prehistoric monuments that we approach today, are not only a testament to a unique prehistoric culture found on the Maltese Islands some 5000 years ago, but they are also a monumental testament to our understanding of the past, the way we have tried to preserve it, and the manner in which we are still interacting with it today.

Bibliography

Abela, G F, 1647 *Della Descrittione di Malta: Isola nel mare Siciliano con le sue antichità, ed altre notittie,* 1984 facsimile of the Malta 1647 edition, Valletta

Adams, A L, 1870 *Notes of a naturalist in the Nile valley and Malta: a narrative of exploration and research in connection with the natural history, geology, and archæology of the lower Nile and Maltese Islands*, Edinburgh

Ashby, T, Bradley, R N, Peet, T E, and Tagliaferro, N, 1913 Excavations in 1908–11 in Various Megalithic Buildings in Malta and Gozo, *Pap Brit Scht Rome* **6** (**1**), 43–109

Baldacchino, J G, 1948 *Annual Report on the Working of the Museum Department, 1947–48*, Malta

Baldacchino, J G, 1949 *Annual Report on the Working of the Museum Department, 1948–49*, Malta

Baldacchino, J G, 1950 *Annual Report on the Working of the Museum Department, 1949–50*, Malta

Baldacchino, J G, 1952 *Annual Report on the Working of the Museum Department, 1950–51*, Malta

Boisgelin de Kerdu, Pierre Marie Louis de, 1804 *Ancient and modern Malta, as also, the history of the knights of St. John of Jerusalem*, London

Bres, O, 1816 *Malta Antica illustrata co' Monumenti, e coll'Istoria*, Rome

Caruana, A A, 1886 *Recent Further Excavations of the Megalithic Antiquities of 'Hagiar-Kim' Malta: Executed in the year 1885 under the direction of Dr A.A. Caruana*, Malta

Cassar, J, 1988 Past Stone Restoration Methods in the Maltese Islands, in V Daniels (ed) *Early Advances in Conservation* British Museum Occasional Papers **65**, London

Ceschi, C, 1939 *Architettura dei templi megalitici di Malta*, Rome

Evans, J D, 1953 The Prehistoric Culture Sequence in the Maltese Archipelago *Proc Prehist Soc* **2**, 41–94

Evans, J D, 1959 *Malta*, London

Evans, J D, 1971 *The Prehistoric Antiquities of the Maltese Islands: A Survey*, London

Houel, J P, 1787 *Voyage Pittoresque des Isles de Sicile, de Malte et de Lipari*, Paris

La Marmora, A, 1836 *Lettre a Monsieur Raoul Rochette, sur le Temple de l'Ile de Gozo*, Paris

Mayr, A, 1901 *Die vorgeschichtlichen Denkmäler von Malta*, München

Mayr, A, 1908 *The Prehistoric Remains of Malta*, Malta

Museums Department, *Archives of the Stone Conservation Laboratory*, National Museums of Archaeology, Malta

Trump, D H, 1966 *Skorba: excavations carried out on behalf of the National Museum of Malta, 1961–1963*, National Museum of Malta & Reports of the Research Committee of the Society of Antiquaries of London, **22**, London & Malta

Ugolini, L M, 1934 *Malta: Origini della civiltà Mediterranea*, {Rome] Italia

Vance, J G, 1840 Hagar Chem or Cham in the Island of Malta: General description of the ruins, *Malta Times* 5th October

Vance, J G, 1842 Description of an Ancient Temple near Crendi, Malta, *Archaeologia* **29**, 227–240

Zammit, T, 1905–07 Archaeological Field-notes, National Museum of Archaeology, Malta

Zammit, T, 1909–12 Archaeological Field-notes, National Museum of Archaeology, Malta

Zammit, T, 1912–17 Archaeological Field-notes, National Museum of Archaeology, Malta

Zammit, T, 1922–24 Archaeological Field-notes, National Museum of Archaeology, Malta

Access and Visibility in Prehistoric Malta

Caroline Malone

MALTA AND ITS MEGALITHIC TEMPLES

Few places in the world offer such potential to explore issues relating to visibility and access in ancient sites as do the Maltese megalithic temples. These remarkable structures are part of the Europe-wide architectural phenomenon of megalith building that occupied much discussion in the 1950s and 1960s (e.g. Daniel 1958; Evans 1953; 1959; 1971; Trump 1961; 1976, 1983; 1995–6; Renfrew 1972; 1973; 1986; 2004) and characterise a late and extremely sophisticated chapter between about 3500 and 2500 BC. Initially recognised in the late 18th century by travellers and antiquarians, speculations about their origins and functions have risen and waned over the decades. Stone structures are notoriously difficult to study, even though they represent some of the most tangible and well-preserved remnants of ancient civilisations long gone. Their dating, reconstruction and interpretation are all challenged by the problems of eroded soils and recent "restorations".

The Maltese temples differ markedly from any other form of megalithic structure in their form and means of access. Simply described, they are formed from multiple lobed chambers around central passages, and in plan look rather like clover leaves. They range from three simple lobes without any central passage or court, to much more complex five, six and more lobes, often with multiple passages linking different parts. They are built from two distinctive local limestones, the hard Coralline which fractures in rough blocks and the soft Globigerina which is cut and shaped to form. Many temple complexes are known across Malta, with concentrations apparently focused around the semi-plains of fertile land that are restricted in extent in the rocky landscapes of the two principal islands, Malta and Gozo (Grima 2005). The temples are clustered in associated groups with two, three and more structures built either adjoining each other, or in close proximity. Some of these are described below, but the most famous are the Ħagar Qim-Mnajdra group, the Skorba-Tá Ħagar Group, the Tarxien group, the Bugibba-Tal Qadi complex and the concentration on Gozo – the Ggantija-Santa Verna-Xewkia group. Although many sites are lost or damaged and difficult to interpret, it seems likely that once there were well in excess of thirty "temple" structures, both isolated and built into adjoining complexes. For a small island of some 325 km^2 such numbers indicate how dense both population and settlement must have been, and how significant were the megalithic structures within Neolithic society.

GIS APPROACHES TO ACCESS AND MONUMENTS

Maltese Temples certainly lend themselves to a variety of spatial studies and modern applications, particular since they have escaped much systematic landscape study until recent times. However, there are very real problems in applying geographical information systems (GIS) to a broad landscape study in areas as densely populated and as devastated by modern settlement and agriculture as those of Malta. Landscape change involving the loss of soil cover, vegetation, and water supplies has meant that a landscape study around monuments is made almost impossible, as a survey of the Xaghra plateau around the Brochtorff Circle and Ggantija has demonstrated (Stoddart pers comm.). The bare bones of the land as presently experienced are probably very different from those of inhabitants five thousand years ago, and frustratingly for archaeologists, the means to extract and interpret such changes seems doomed (Malone et al. forthcoming). Stratified soils, organic preservation of biological indicators or, indeed, soil in its original setting are all extremely difficult to locate in an eroded rocky landscape where all soil must be reserved and spread from building sites, thus muddling and confusing the location of archaeological material catastrophically.

Although the environment is a difficult aspect to study, the standing monuments still clearly have much potential since they remain where they were built and more or less in the same form. Research over the years has focused on their form, and the development sequence of architecture and the relationship of pottery style to the broader architectural and cultural phases (Evans 1953; Trump 1995–6, 2004). Research has concentrated on catalogues (e.g. Evans 1971), rather than explore how the structures worked as buildings with many levels of visibility and accessibility.

GIS applied at a much more modest site-orientated scale has not been tested on these sites before and presents a new challenge for studying Maltese temples. Work attempted in Malta, employing both GIS and Quicktime (digital 360 degree photo-studies), has shown there is great potential for using landscape approaches at a micro-scale for assessing how sites were located within their immediate landscape and how they might have been accessed and seen. Recent preoccupations with sensory archaeology (Bradley 2000; Tilley 1994; 2004, Watson and Keating 1999) are bolstered by the evidence provided by these studies, as they enable us to revisit, reassess and re-experience a site from various angles and in different conditions. Michael Anderson undertook a series of Quicktime studies, following an earlier exercise of GIS work from drawn plans of several Maltese temples, which provides much of the stimulus for this new approach to visibility work and with fruitful outcomes.

VISIBILITY – CONCEPTS ABOUT WHAT WE SEE, TEMPLE AND TOMB

Maltese Temples, in the evolved and complex state at least, are focused around a large open arena, on to which the central passages of the structures open. These areas range from small paved courtyards, barely 15m wide by 10m deep as at Kordin III, to immense open areas over 50m wide and as many metres deep between different buildings as at Ggantija and Ħagar Qim. The courtyards or 'stages' for public performance are very important parts of the layout of the temple complexes, since it is the courtyards that provided the arena for participation, performance and display.

The interiors of the temples, however, appear to have been closed and inaccessible to most onlookers. We know that access into the temple structures was controlled, since each entrance into the internal rooms or lobes of the structures was barred and closed by doors or wooden barriers inserted into holes drilled into the upright stone door-jambs. Even within the temples, the different 'rooms' and passages were barred one from another, suggesting that privacy, secrecy and notions about sacred, ritual space and social hierarchy were underlying principles in the layout and use of the buildings. As will become clear in the later sections, spaces were used for specific storage and activity purposes, and the placement of artefacts, which were often closely associated with laterality and position within the site. In terms of access, the Maltese sites represent thresholds into other cognitive worlds, and they mediate between the hierarchical world of the living, the dead, deities and ancestors. These rather abstract claims can be supported through an appreciation of the art objects and their relationship with the precise structure and their placement. To explore these ideas, three sites are discussed below.

TARXIEN, MALTA (FIG. 1)

Most of the Maltese temples were cleared in the 19th century, with little record made of archaeological sediments or collapsed structures. The ruined remains seen today are often considerably reconstructed, and much vital information has been lost that would have enabled understanding of original structure and function. The exception to this is the site of Tarxien where Themistocles Zammit, the first director of the Museum of Malta, excavated from 1914–17 (Zammit 1929, 1930). Whilst scanty in detail in comparison to modern archaeological standards, this work nevertheless stands the test of time, enabling modern scholars to piece together many

of the component parts. In particular, Zammit recorded the location of cult objects, which has provided a base from which to compare finds from recent excavations. The findspots of numerous caches of 'ritual' and cult material, figurines, axes, phallic objects, bowls and hearths were mapped and the distribution of these can be seen on Figure 1.

This site is considered to be late in the architectural development of the Temple Culture, and consists of three main temples, two set side by side, and a larger one in front, cutting across the approach to the intermediate although later temple set behind it. Smaller, ruined structures lay to the east, and a large forecourt with distinctive libation hole slabs at either side, lay to the west. The extent of the site has never been fully explored or exposed, and it is today hemmed in by modern development. However, it is clear that it formed part of a wider complex including the Kordin temple group, Ħal Saflieni and other temple structures on the plateau over-looking the Grand Harbour of Valletta to the east. The plateau is located on Globigerina limestone enabling the ready supply of building stone.

GGANTIJA, XAGHRA, GOZO

Often cited as the oldest of the Temples, the Ggantija is a rugged construction of coralline limestone, located close to the Brochtorff Circle on the Xaghra plateau of Gozo. It was cleared in the early 19th century and detailed drawings survive showing the internal structures as they were first encountered. The pair of temples opened to the south east onto a vast semi-circular forecourt that was built up on an artificial terrace. Within the temples, Globigerina limestone door jambs, thresholds, paved floors, altars, steps and wall-lining reverse the rugged exterior to one of sophisticated and highly finished detail. Very few objects were recorded from the early excavations, so location of material is not possible, even though the visible appearance was recorded (Grima 2004) (Fig. 2). The structural evolution of the site is problematic, since the underlying floors indicate an early beginning, but the relationship of these to the freestanding walls of the super-structure are difficult to date. The complex of Ggantija relates to a number of sites on the southern edge of the Xaghra plateau, and these include Santa Verna and the Brochtorff Circle as well as caves and ruined structures. Modern development has destroyed much of the coherence of the early landscape.

BROCHTORFF'S XAGHRA CIRCLE, GOZO

Excavations between 1987 and 1994 (Malone *et al.* 1993; forthcoming) revealed not a temple but a second funerary hypogeum, echoing the discovery of the Ħal Saflieni Hypogeum in the early years of the 20th century. However, the Circle site was a natural cave in Coralline limestone, and contained damaged but nevertheless plentiful remains of burials and

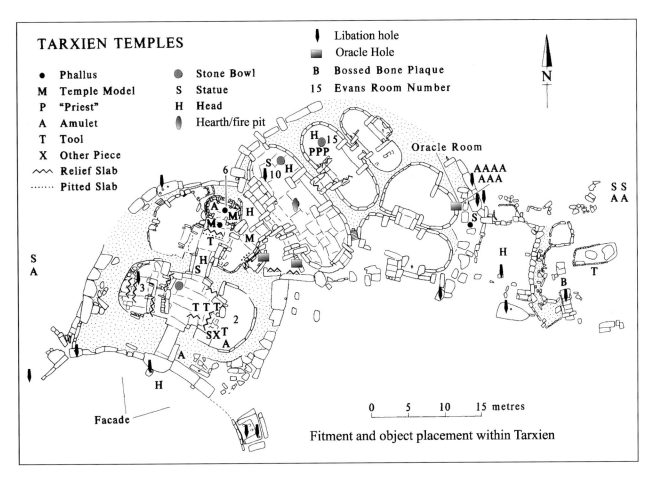

Figure 1   Tarxien: Plan showing features and locations of artefacts.

associated grave-goods, cult material and structure. Encircled by a megalithic wall, the enclosed site incorporated surface structures and a massive threshold that formed a ceremonial entrance to the underlying caves. These extended at least 30m into a series of caverns, the full of extent of which have not been determined. The rugged natural rock was enhanced by imported Globigerina limestone set as altars, steps, roof supports and grave-markers. Several different zones within the caves were marked out by stone structures around natural recesses to form burial compartments, which on excavation contained distinctive arrangements of body parts and objects (see Malone *et al.* forthcoming). The site was in use from the Zebbug period to the end of the Tarxien Temple Period around 2450 BC. Thereafter, catastrophic roof collapse and abandonment, Bronze Age re-occupation and more recent disturbance have all caused damage and muddle to the archaeological deposits, which nevertheless are still the most comprehensively studied from any temple period site in Malta.

DEVELOPMENT OF ACCESS – ZEBBUG PERIOD

Major construction and building of durable remains began it seems in the Zebbug period, around 4000 BC

in Malta, and for this period we have rock cut tombs and indistinct buildings. Most Temple Period sites have deposits and vague stone structures from the Zebbug phase and its immediate successor, the Mgarr, but ceremonial architecture is difficult to identify, even though small lobed constructions may have been evolving. The Ggantija phase around 3600–3200 BC seems to be the first phase of major construction in the evolution of Maltese temples and elements of structures apparently relating to the period are also know at several temple sites, as well as at the Hypogea. However, it does appear that much of the major rebuilding, enlargement and enhancement of temple structures relates to the full and late Temple Period, from Saflieni to Tarxien – 3300–2450 BC – if indeed these phases, which are entirely related to a ceramic sequence, can be trusted. Certainly the new information from the Brochtorff Circle and the dated human remains (rather than stray scraps of carbonised material in sediment) suggest that much new building and redesign was a feature of the final centuries of the Temple Culture. For this paper, I would argue that the issues of controlled access, ritual specialists, sophisticated art objects and decorated stonework relate specifically to this final, if long, phase of development.

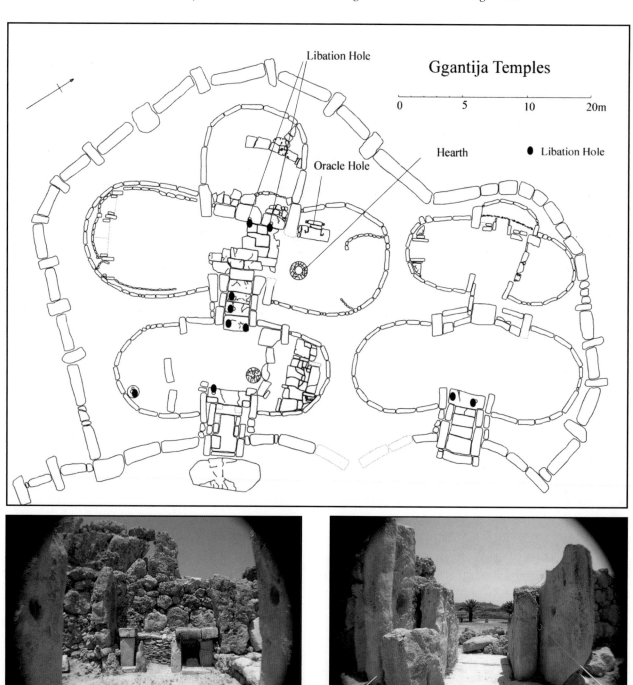

Figure 2   Ggantija: Plan showing features, and photographs showing views (a) inside and (b) outside.

TEMPLE PERIOD ACCESS

Our study of temple access begins with the general approaches of GIS to landscape, and sees these applied instead to sites and their immediate surroundings. The complexity of the Maltese temples enables GIS studies on access and structural depth to be employed with confidence, and offers the possibility to compare these with each other and over time. GIS has mostly been employed to bolster environmental determinism across physical landscapes, but here we use it as a tool to examine landscapes and structures of power and ideology. As in landscape studies, the application of cost-surface analysis provides a means to examine and measure levels of access into the built structures, and we have employed Hillier and Hanson access models of internal structures to this end (see in particular Anderson 2005). We have also focused on visibility which in most landscape-focused work has been on viewsheds, but here we employ multiple viewsheds of architecture. The techniques that describe this work are detailed in Anderson and Stoddart (forthcoming) but the principles of eRRA or extended Real Relative Assymmetry underlie the work as does cumulative architectural integration, which has been extended to take into account the actual shape of the internal spaces, or rooms. A successful model of this approach is seen in access modelling of Pompeian houses (Anderson 2005). In essence, this established view-sheds from key fixed points, and enabled a grid of viewsheds to overlie this from numerous points, thus offering the possibility of reconstructing the 'view' of the internal space of these complex structures, and perhaps, an appreciation of the original access into the spaces.

Application of this approach to the Tarxien temple, which is certainly the most complex of the temple agglomerations is instructive (Fig. 3). Whilst complex, it is also internally well integrated, and the lines of internal activity, movement and storage indicate a well coordinated ritual space. In addition, the site contains numerous very secret, hidden or private areas, which are outside the lines of visibility or general access.

In comparison, the Ggantija Temple, which may follow an earlier and simpler layout is much less complex. The front court for example is the most 'integrated' of any temple site, and provides clear views of the entire façade and entries into the two temple structures. The integration continues into the interior of the two structures, with corridors leading straight into the lobed spaces and these offer direct lines of sight to the altars and structures ahead. However, whilst direct, the deeper or more remote areas of each lobed space contain the bulk of detailed decorative devices that enhanced the inner space of the temple. Put crudely, there is a marked contrast between areas of visibility and invisibility, exterior and interior, and between the different materials that define these spaces (Fig. 4).

The hypogea of Brochtorff and Hal Saflieni present much more complexity in terms of determining visibility and accessibility even though perhaps the same principles apply. These sites were both invisible, in that they were subterranean, dark, secret places. Access in the two known examples was through one entrance that led through and down tortuous steps and passages, through controlled 'doors', and finally into deep spaces. The Hal Saflieni Hypogeum is almost entirely a man-made structure, quarried out of natural Globigerina rock, combining forms that reflect both a natural cave and a built temple. It grew organically over numerous levels – three major ones, and five if the deep recesses that reach over 10m below ground level are included – and it contained some 30–40 individual spaces, niches and chambers, most of which were used for burial or ritual storage.

The Brochtorff Circle (Fig. 5) differs considerably from Hal Saflieni, in that the parent rock is Coralline, rugged and natural, and the internal space of the caves was adapted and modified by imported constructions. These include steps set into the cave walls to enable access, threshold steps separating different 'chambers', niches and rooms within the caves, upright megalithic screen constructions that obscured the natural character of the caves together with sophisticated altars, wall niches, trilithon doors, portholes and the like, which parallel temple building devices. The placement of bowls, oracle holes, storage and secret places also seem to reflect the same rules of laterality and position within both sites.

To argue whether the natural modified cave inspired the man-made, or vice-versa, is probably pointless, and instead, the recognition that subterranean space was organised following the same structural rules as the above-ground temples is important. Our current studies are suggesting that the subterranean spaces mirror the above-ground temples, with similar placement of special ritual paraphernalia such as bowls, oracle holes, storage places and ritual areas. Certainly, now that studies of the Brochtorff Circle on Gozo are reaching a conclusion, and valid comparison with other sites is now possible, it seems clear that the ritual structures, whether intended for life or death rituals, followed strict rules of laterality and position, and that ceremonies were conducted according to these rules. The remnants of structure thus might be clues to some of this lost complexity.

OBJECT DISTRIBUTIONS, VISIBILITY AND THE EMERGENCE OF INDIVIDUAL AND COLLECTIVE IDENTITY

The association of prehistoric objects within secure archaeological contexts are rare, and the old finds are problematic, but Maltese sites, burial ones especially, offer potential for analysis. The recording of material was haphazard until the Tarxien excavations, but these together with the Brochtorff Circle discoveries, support some generalisations. At Tarxien, as Figure 1 shows, the distribution of ritual objects indicates some distinct patterns. For example, phalli are generally placed in the deeper places on the left, tools for sacrifice together with altars dedicated to offerings seem to be placed on the right, along with hearths that are on the right or directly ahead. The most decorative rooms with reliefs are usually on the left whilst oracle holes, often filled with 'posted' amulets, are on the right. There are many more such associations and patterns, currently under study by the Cambridge Templeton Project.

Progression through these cult places clearly involved, just as contemporary worship involves, special activities in particular places. Therefore, it might be claimed that we can begin to predict where particularly visible objects of cult paraphernalia were displayed and thus might be found in a temple site. However, burial contexts add complexity, with

Figure 3   Tarxien: High and low visibility areas. Examples of images and vistas: (a) large bowl in SW temple; (b) view through SW temple; (c) large standing statue; (d) decorated altars and bowl on left side of SW temple; (e) libation trough and (f) male animal frieze.

a greater range of grave goods and material than is found in the temples.

Zebbug period burials (c 4000–3600 BC) contain rather mundane objects, shell bead necklaces and shell pendants, bone pendants, axes and axe amulets, pottery (often containing quantities of red ochre), obsidian and chert tools, and in two instances stone 'menhir' anthropomorphic grave markers. The collective ritual of burial that took place in small a-forno rock cut tombs has meant that nearly all the original association of objects has been lost in a general mixing of deposits as bodies were

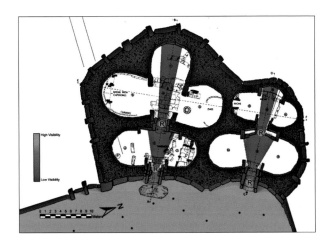

Figure 4   Ggantija: Plan showing levels of access.

successively introduced into the tomb. No open ritual or temple site has recovered any indications of Zebbug activity that can be interpreted, and the burial ritual remains the principal source of knowledge for this period.

Ritual objects for the succeeding phases of Ggantija (c 3600–3200 BC) and Saflieni (c 3200–3000 BC) are also rather obscure, even though assumptions have been made in the past about the early development of Temple period style and cult. However, it is not clear that there is much evidence that is securely linked to Ggantija, and the two sculpted heads and the snake relief found at the type site may well belong to full Temple Period occupation rather than the early period. Therefore it is only possible really to talk of the Temple Period and Tarxien for the purposes of interpreting ritual behaviour, and the Brochtorff Circle especially provides solid dated evidence for this period. Elaboration and growing sophistication of many aspects of material culture characterise the period. Pottery becomes standardised with offering bowls and a range of decorated and plain vessels (Evans 1953). Personal ornaments change in form and material, and figurative objects become frequent, modelled from clay

Figure 5   Brochtorff Circle megaliths.

into the characteristic 'obese' and semi-realistic figurines of various sizes. These range from very small intimate objects placed with the dead or secreted into temple caches, to intermediate public statuettes as seen in the 'Priest' and 'Sleeping Lady' figures, to enormous life-size sculptures at Tarxien and Ta Silg (Frendo and Bonnano 1997; Vella 1999). Other objects include chert knives and other lithics, phallic representations in free-standing and relief forms, stone bowls of various sizes for ritual cleansing or drinking, small altars and special carved stones and niches, palettes and bowls, representations of animals and monsters in clay and stone, and a variety of natural and man-made amulet-type objects that appear to have value and meaning. The main change from early to late in this sequence is from intimate objects for personal decoration, to much more symbolic public objects, presented within a collective ritual. The role of the individual thus changes subtly from one where the persona of an individual is subsumed within the collective clan identity, to one where the persona remains individual but the object representations become part of a wider collective identity. Ancestors may be represented in portraits of the individuals suggested through art objects and their identity and status begin to take on new significance as details of hair, dress, postures and identity both conform and diverge from a standard style.

SITE ANATOMY AND ACCESS

Access into a funerary site is necessarily constrained. Entry means crossing a sensory barrier from living space to one of decomposing bodies, dry bones and the almost universal sense of separation that exists between spaces for the living and the dead. In Malta we see the a growing sense of formal separation developing from the early rock cut tombs to the massive collective hypogea set within special enclosures (see Malone *et al.* 1995). No doubt early cemeteries of tombs were marked on the surface by signals of some type, but the Brochtorff Circle in its developed phase employed a massive megalithic wall to separate the living world from that of the dead (Fig. 6). From the moment of entry, to the final deposition of a corpse, the enclosure separated the funerary actions from the surrounding environment, demanding passage over several layers of visible, physical and sensory thresholds.

A funerary procession would have entered the site through the massive stone pillars set into the eastern side of the Circle, aligned to a path that led directly to the Ggantija temple to the east. Remnant megaliths still remain, indicating that the route was formalised. Once inside the Circle, the path appears to have led directly to a massive threshold structure located on the edge of the cave access, which probably included a large trilithon entrance, with altars and offering tables at either side. Significantly, at either side of the threshold, there were pits containing large numbers of arranged human remains and some intact skeletons. The human remains were

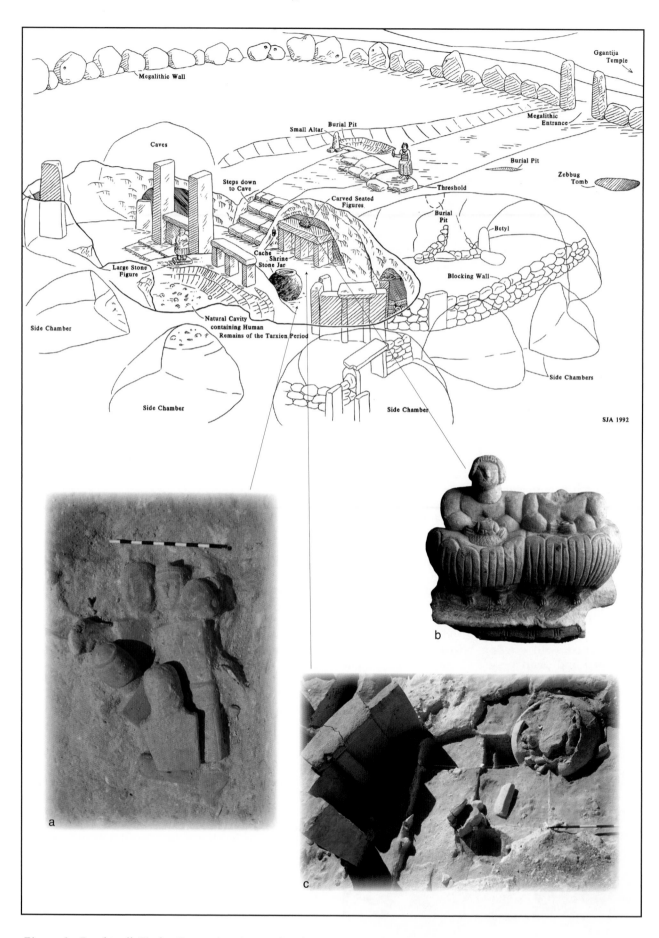

Figure 6   Brochtorff Circle: Composite picture showing reconstruction drawing, (a) cache of semi-excavated figures, (b) figurine of carved seated figures and (c) semi-aerial view of shrine megaliths.

carefully stacked, and the pits covered and cobbled. Passing over the threshold involved passing over the 'ancestors' buried there. No doubt some memory of this remained throughout the life of the site, so that the passage into the world of the dead was punctuated by distinct crossing points – as reference to the ancestors.

Once over the threshold, steps led down into the caves, and remnants of the steps and of structures that probably supported a quite elaborate entry have been recorded. At the bottom on the steps, heaps of skulls were found derived from stacked displays on stone shelves, suggesting that the visitor encountered a very visible reminder of the dead, at the moment of passing into the dark subterranean caves. In turn, this zone led to others, each differentially marked by structures, organisation of burial space, offerings and forms of burial, and at the centre of the western cave, a carefully constructed area surrounding a huge stone bowl, about a metre in height and diameter (Fig. 7). Around this so-called Shrine, Globigerina megaliths were set up forming screens on all sides with entry points into the more distant zones of the caves. Significantly, all the most sophisticated art objects were found closely associated with this zone. Initially, few burials were placed in the area, but as time went on, and the caves filled, layer upon layer of burial were inserted. There are close parallels to the arrangements in Ħal Saflieni, where a central chamber with screens cut from the rock surround the ceremonial space, and significantly, a round cavity for a stone bowl is also cut into one edge. Close by, a deep covered pit contained significant ritual art objects, parallel again to the discoveries made at the Circle. (Figs 3 and 5).

Beyond the central Shrine area, the Circle contained many additional caves and passages, now all damaged and confused by the collapse of the cave roof and subsequent disturbance. These zones included a deep cavity, marked by crude megaliths that appear to have supported additional structures, and which was filled by discarded human remains moved from other areas of the site. Niches at the sides were marked off by megalithic slabs and rough stone walls, with distinct burial areas set behind them. Whilst the site is still incompletely excavated, it seems clear that many different actions took place in the rites of burial, with initial deposition, later removal of skulls and long bones for rearrangement elsewhere, the disposal of certain body parts into dump areas, and the deliberate selection and arrangement of some body parts to appear as if complete, but derived from many individuals in small pits in the floor.

Around the whole, built structures were erected, modified, collapsed and rebuilt, often in part to try and support a crumbling cave roof. Some areas became filled during the life of the site, making them inaccessible and invisible. The dark and ever-filling environment presented a changing experience during its thousand-year use. Ritual action, modified by the memory of how to undertake funerary ceremonies, was in part directed by the distinctive

layout of both temple and tomb where certain actions were undertaken in particular places. Some were on the right, others on the left, regardless of the detailed layout of the site, and always, purification in the bowl, or libation in a hole/pit, or offering on an altar remained set actions (Malone forthcoming).

PATTERNS OF DISTINCTION

The placement of artefacts and special objects within this curiously conservative environment indicates that this action too was directed and deliberate. However, the Circle burials reveal that different groups were furnished with distinctly different objects, both over time, and between areas of the site. For example, Zebbug burials enjoyed shell bead necklaces and pendants, but no figurative statuettes. In the later phases, terracotta figurines were often placed with dead, but necklaces were few. Offering bowls and small miniature pots for ochre were also frequent grave goods, and ochre was liberally spread over particular individuals, and not others. With some, particularly the individuals who were buried close to the stone bowl, small greenstone axe-amulets were found. However, disturbances even during prehistoric use meant that few items remained associated with the original bearer and remain difficult to interpret conclusively.

THE RITE OF PASSAGE: SOME CONCLUSIONS

As argued above, the entire Circle, like the Temples, appears to have been laid out with precision and purpose, and it employed massive modification of the natural space provided by the rugged caves to provide a visible access into the world of the dead. The temples with their thresholds and hidden interiors may also represent access to the realm of deities and ancestors, but for the living more than for the dead. Layout both internally and externally conformed to long-held practice and belief. Recent studies for example have demonstrated how some sites (in particular Manijdra) were orientated towards astronomical events, and cosmology must lie behind the complexity that even remains today (Stoddart *et al.* 1993). Much has been claimed about a priestly hierarchy in early Malta, and this proposition remains a viable one, when account is taken of the controlling arrangements that both temples and tombs embodied. No one simply walked into these sites. There were barriers at every stage, doors, screens, thresholds, which at each point seem to have required an offering (in libation holes or on altars), subservience to superiors (bowing to enter under low doorways and portholes, submission at oracle holes, confrontation with ancestor-deities), purification (through cleansing in the stone bowls, through burning of materials in hearths), sacrifice (slaughter of animals and presentation of food and goods), not to mention taboos and notions long since lost. Access to the deeper zones, whether vertical or horizontal, of the temple sites probably reflected greater degrees

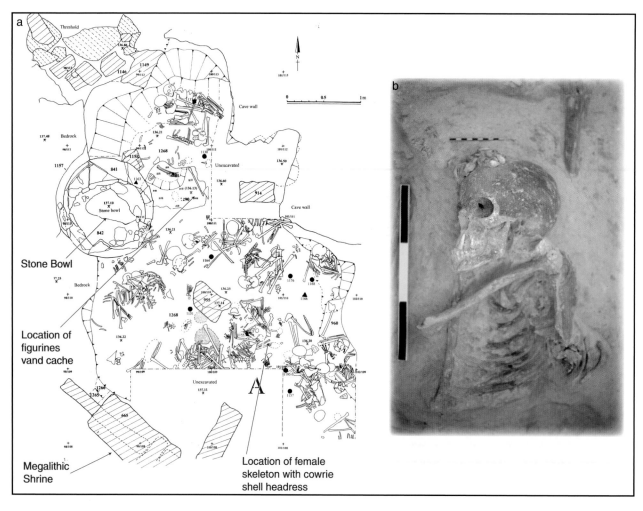

Figure 7   Brochtorff Circle: (a) plan of 'shrine' with stone bowl and bones and (b) photograph of the ochred 'cowrie' lady skeleton.

of enlightenment or status in the individuals and groups involved. Such spaces also seem to have been reserved for the most significant objects and activities. Despite the scanty remnants, new research is suggesting novel avenues for further interpretation of how ritual operated in early Malta.

Bibliography

Anderson, M, 2005 *Visitors, inhabitants, space and power in the Pomepiian house*. Unpublished doctoral thesis, Cambridge University

Anderson, M, and Stoddart, S, forthcoming Mapping cult contexts: GIS applications in Maltese temples, in Malone and Barrowclough forthcoming

Bradley, R,. 2000 *The Archaeology of Natural Places*, London, Routledge

Daniel, G, 1958 The megalith builders of western Europe, London, Hutchinson

Evans, J D, 1953 The prehistoric culture sequence of the Maltese archipelago. *Proc Prehist Soc* **19**, 41–94

Evans, J D, 1959 *Malta*, London

Evans, J D, 1971 *The prehistoric antiquities of the Maltese islands: a survey*. London, Athlone Press

Frendo, A, J, and Bonanno, A, 1997 Excavations at Tas-Silg, 1996. *Malta Archaeological Review* **2**, 8–10

Grima, R, 2004 *The Archaeological Drawings of Charles Fredrick de Brochtorff*. Malta, Midsea Books Ltd and Heritage Malta

Grima, R, 2005 *Monuments in search of a landscape: The landscape context of monumentality in Late Neolithic Malta*, Unpublished doctoral dissertation of the University of London

Malone, C, forthcoming Space, Structure and Art in prehistoric Malta, in Malone and Barrowclough forthcoming

Malone, C, and Barraclough, D (eds) forthcoming *Cult in Context*, Conference Proceedings, Oxford, Oxbow

Malone, C, Bonanno, A, Gouder, T, Stoddart, S, and Trump, D, 1993 The Death Cults of prehistoric Malta, *Scientific American* **269** (**6**), 110–117

Malone, C, Stoddart, S, Trump, D, Bonanno, A, and Gouder, T, in press, *The Brochtorff Circle excavations and their environs*, Cambridge, McDonald Institute monographs. 2007

Malone, C, Stoddart, S, Trump, D, Bonanno, A, and Pace, A, (eds) 2006 *Mortuary ritual in prehistoric*

Malta. The Brochtorff Circle excavations (1987–1994). Cambridge, McDonald Institute

Renfrew, A C, 1972 Malta and the calibrated radiocarbon chronology, *Antiquity* **46** (**182**), 141–144.

Renfrew, A C, 1973 *Before Civilisation,* London, Jonathan Cape.

Renfrew, A C, 1986 The prehistoric Maltese achievement and its interpretation, in A Bonanno (ed), *Archaeology and fertility cult in the Ancient Mediterranean,* Amsterdam, Gruner Publishing Co, pp. 118–13

Renfrew, A C, 2004. Islands Out of Time? Towards an analytical framework, in S M Fitzpatrick (ed), *Voyages of Discovery. The archaeology of islands.* London, Praeger, 275–294

Stoddart, S, Bonanno, A, Gouder, T, Malone, C, and Trump, D, 1993 Cult in an Island Society: Prehistoric Malta in the Tarxien period, *Cambridge Archaeol J* **3** (**1**), 3–19

Tilley, C, 1994 *A Phenomenology of Landscape,* Oxford, Berg

Tilley, C, 2004 *The Materiality of Stone: explorations in Landscape Phenomenology,* Oxford, Berg

Trump, D, 1961 The later prehistory of Malta, *Proc Prehist Soc* **27**, 253–262

Trump, D, 1976 The collapse of the Maltese temples, in G Sieveking, I H Longworth and K E Wilson (eds), *Problems in Economic and Social Archaeology,* London, Duckworth, 605–610

Trump, D, 1983 Megalithic architecture in Malta, in A C Renfrew (ed), *The megalithic monuments of Western Europe,* London, Thames and Hudson, 64–76

Trump, D, 1995–6 Radiocarbon dates from Malta, *Accordia Research Papers* **6**, 173–178.

Trump, D, 2004 Dating Malta's Prehistory, in D Cilia (ed), *Malta Before History,* Malta, Miranda, 230–241

Watson, A, and Keating, D, 1999 Architecture and sound: an acoustic analysis of megalithic monuments in prehistoric Britain, *Antiquity* **73** (**280**), 325–36

Vella, N C, 1999 "Trunkless legs of stone": debating ritual continuity at Tas-Silg, Malta, in A Mifsud and C Savona-Ventura (eds), *Facets of Maltese Prehistory,* Malta, The Prehistoric Society of Malta, 225–239

Zammit, T, 1929 *The Neolithic Temples of Ħal-Tarxien-Malta. A short description of the monuments with plan and illustrations,* Valletta, Empire Press

Zammit, T, 1930 *Prehistoric Malta, the Tarxien Temples,* Oxford & London, Oxford University Press & London University Press

Avebury World Heritage Site:
Megaliths, Management Plans and Monitoring

Melanie Pomeroy-Kellinger

This paper aims to explore a number of themes relating to developments in the Avebury World Heritage Site (WHS) over the last few years. The first part of the paper introduces the key components of the WHS, and the management and ownership context. It then explores the development of the site management plans and other management projects. The second part of the paper is devoted to an analysis of the strengths and weaknesses of Avebury as a WHS, and the successes and failures in its management. It concludes with an outline of suggested priorities for the future management of site.

THE WORLD HERITAGE SITE

Stonehenge and Avebury in Wiltshire, England, (Fig. 1) were nominated together onto the World Heritage List in 1986 because they present the largest stone circle in the world (Avebury) and the most sophisticated (Stonehenge). Moreover, both stone circles are within cultural landscapes with outstanding concentrations of ritual and ceremonial monuments dating from the Neolithic and Bronze Age. Although inscribed as a single WHS because of their similar archaeological monuments, the two sites are located forty kilometres apart. The two parts of the WHS are currently managed separately, each having its own WHS management plan, research framework and World Heritage Site Officer. Since the 1986 inscription, there have been discussions and debates about the merits of the joint nomination and the similarities and difference between the two areas.

BOUNDARIES AND OWNERSHIP

The Avebury WHS is located on the Marlborough Downs in North Wiltshire.

The WHS boundary encloses some twenty-two square kilometres (2,200 hectares) of prime agricultural land. It contains around 330 known archaeological monuments (mainly prehistoric earthworks), a third of which are considered to be of national importance (Scheduled Monuments). The World Heritage designation was achieved because six of the monuments are considered to be of international significance. The Henge, West Kennet Avenue, West Kennet Long Barrow, Windmill Hill, Silbury Hill, and The Sanctuary are all in state care (guardianship) and open to the public (Fig. 2).

It has been acknowledged for several years that the boundaries of the Avebury WHS, as defined in the 1985 Nomination Document, are inadequate in several places. This reflects the fact that the boundary was drawn up using map-based information only and omitted observation on the ground. Moreover, several archaeological discoveries made since 1985 in locations close to, or straddling, the boundary, have promoted calls for its reassessment and revision. Consequently, a detailed assessment was undertaken and the most recent management plan for Avebury (2005) contains recommendations for changes to the boundary, amounting to a proposed increase of 10% of the current total area. These recommendations will have to be endorsed by the Department for Culture, Media and Sport (DCMS) and forwarded to UNESCO for approval. The issue of inadequate boundaries is common to several other WH sites in the UK, including Stonehenge, as flagged up in the UNESCO 2005 Periodic Reporting questionnaires compiled by site managers for the DCMS.[1]

As with the majority of WH sites in the UK, Avebury is not in single ownership. The largest landowner is the National Trust, which owns and manages the central third of the WHS area. This ownership by the Trust is a very positive means of ensuring the long-term future of the main monuments. In addition to the National Trust, there are a dozen other landowners who own land in the WHS. Most of them farm the land or use it for racehorse training, and all have their own objectives and aspirations for the area.

Indeed, one of the major challenges for the management of the WHS is the fact that sixty-percent of the area within its boundary is still in arable cultivation. This has an impact on the survival and condition of many of the earthworks in the area, though progress is being made on taking out of cultivation areas with the most vulnerable archaeological sites. This is being achieved through agri-environmental grant schemes and other management agreements.

There are four villages within the WHS (Avebury, Avebury Trusloe, West Kennett, Beckhampton) and one (West Overton) which is part in and part out of the WHS boundary. Together the villages host a community of several hundred people who are represented by two parish councils on the various WHS working groups.

Avebury village itself has since early times had a symbiotic relationship with the prehistoric Henge

---

[1] Periodic Reporting is UNESCO's participatory exercise to collect information relating to World Heritage Sites on a regional, national and site basis. The first round of reporting on UK sites was undertaken in 2005 and it will be repeated on a six-yearly cycle.

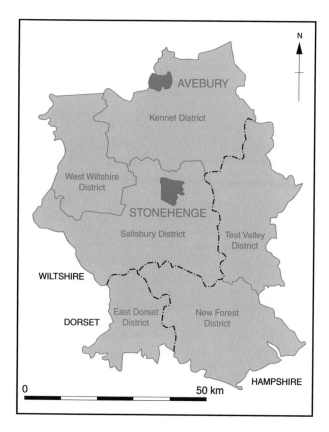

Figure 1 Location of Avebury and Stonehenge in Wiltshire.

and Stone Circle and this is still evident today (Fig. 3). The village was first established in the Saxon period, with the earliest buildings (such as St James Church) being built just outside of the prehistoric monument. Gradually the village extended into and beyond the other side of the monument. Many of the village buildings have been built using bits of sarsen stone, some undoubtedly taken from the standing stones, many of which were broken up in the medieval period and later. Alexander Keiller reversed the trend when he took down many of the village buildings during his large-scale archaeological excavation and restoration programme in the 1930s and 1940s.

LOCAL COMMUNITIES, VISITORS AND EROSION

Keiller's restoration work was largely responsible for the visibility of the prehistoric remains we see today and the great visitor interest in Avebury. It is difficult in Avebury to get an accurate count of visitor numbers, because, unlike Stonehenge, it is a free site with open access and has multiple entrances. However, it seems that visitor numbers grew from the post-war period, reaching a peak of around 350,000 annual visitors in the mid 1990s. Although visitor numbers do appear to have subsequently tapered to just fewer than 300,000 in the last five

years (according to counts undertaken by the National Trust) visitors are still the key source of frustration for the local community.

The influx of visitors to Avebury, particularly in the summer and during holiday periods, certainly does impact on village life. Parking congestion caused by visitors parking in the village is a major cause of complaint. The biggest cause for concern is the influx of sometimes several thousand visitors during the mid-summer solstice period and for other pagan festivals throughout the year. Over the solstice period the main visitor car park becomes full of vehicles for several days and nights as the area becomes an unofficial caravan and camp site. This causes problems for the National Trust, who try to control the amount of camping on their land, because camping is against their own by-laws. It also causes health and hygiene concerns for the local villagers whose lives are disrupted by the late-night noise of revellers and whose gardens are used as toilets by solstice visitors, for whom there are insufficient facilities.

As well as causing difficulties for local people, the large numbers of visitors have had a significant impact on the condition of the key monuments open to public access, and in particular on the Henge. Erosion scars can be seen at almost all of the key access point onto the Henge bank and along its top (Fig. 4). Erosion is most pronounced at the ends of the steepest banks where the soil cover is thin. The National Trust have an on-going programme of erosion repair and management involving the replacement of worn turf and closing off of the repaired and vulnerable areas at certain times of year.

Until recently, the visitor experience of Avebury (in terms of the interpretation of the site) had change little since the 1930s. Avebury is unique for a WHS in having the archaeological collections from the excavations of its key sites housed and displayed on site. The Alexander Keiller Museum opened in the 1930s to display Keiller's discoveries from his large-scale excavations in the Henge, West Kennet Avenue and Windmill Hill. Housed in an old Stable Block, the Museum is small and has a limited amount of display space. In an attempt to improve the provision of interpretation, the National Trust have now successfully converted the Grade 1 listed Barn adjacent to the Museum into the Barn Gallery Exhibition. The Barn, dating from the 1680s, was originally part of the Manor Farm complex but more recently and until 1998 was used as a museum of Rural Life. The National Trust has succeeded in overcoming several constraints, such as the need to protect the historic fabric of the building and to accommodate rare protected bats within the roof space, to restore the barn. The barn was opened to visitors in 2001. Visitors are now able to appreciate its historic and cathedral-like space at the same time as experiencing an exhibition on the Avebury landscape and its archaeology.

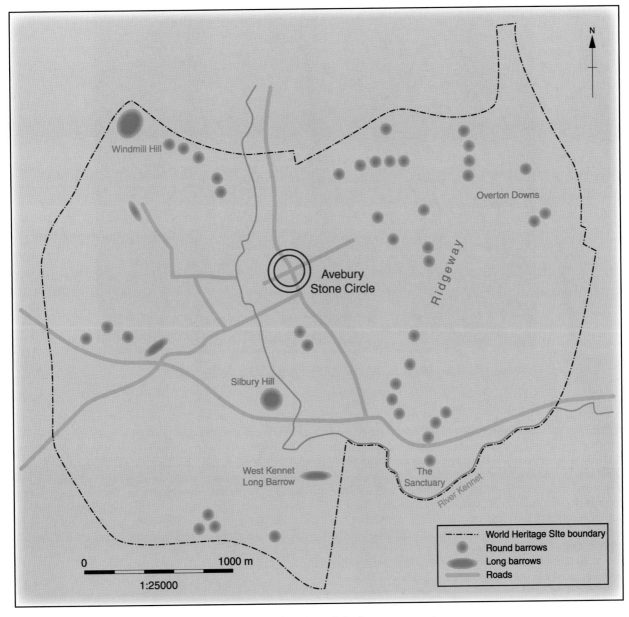

Figure 2   Map of the Avebury WHS showing the location of the key monuments.

MANAGEMENT PLANS

UNESCO now requires that management plans are submitted together with the nomination document for sites wishing to be inscribed onto the World Heritage List, but this was not the case for the earliest sites inscribed, including UK sites such as Stonehenge and Avebury nominated in the 1980s. Since the mid-1990s the UK Government has been encouraging the development of such plans for sites already on the List.

The process of developing the first management plan for Avebury began in 1996 with funding from English Heritage and took two years to complete. It was revised and re-published in 2005 and will continue to be reviewed on a six-yearly cycle (in line with UNESCOs Periodic Reporting cycle). A number of key

studies were commissioned to support the development of the plan, including visitor and traffic management reports and a landscape assessment. There was a good deal of consultation and local community involvement during the development of the plan.

This initial management plan became out of date quickly due to significant new archaeological discoveries in the Avebury landscape (see below) and because of changes in land use and management. Work began on revising the plan in 2004 and it was obvious from the start of the process that much of it had to be revised or changed. It was identified that over sixty percent of the objectives set out in 1998 had been achieved and new objectives needed to be included in the revised plan.

The revised plan was more succinct and sophisticated, and less idealistic than the first one. It reflected

Figure 3   Avebury Henge and Stone Circle: Aerial view looking North.

the better understanding of the landscape that resulted from excavations and studies undertaken in the previous five years. It included recommendations for boundary changes and for monitoring inzdicators, as well as a greater emphasises on the implementation of objectives and priority actions. The public consultation exercise on this second plan evoked a larger response than the earlier one, particularly from local people.

A number of conclusions can be drawn from the development of the two plans for Avebury. The key conclusion is that it is the development process,

rather than the physical existence of the management plan, which is most important in terms of building the consensus and partnerships necessary for the management of a site like Avebury. Avebury also demonstrates that much can happen in five years to change our understanding of the site and how it should be managed. Therefore, management plans need to be flexible and easy to update on a regular basis.

RESEARCH AGENDA

It has long been recognised that the Avebury landscape has a high potential for the discovery of new archaeological sites, especially through aerial photography. It has been demonstrated by the identification of at least sixty new sites between 1997 and 2004. Many of these sites are ploughed out barrows or enclosures of various periods, identified though English Heritage's National Mapping Programme of the Avebury area (English Heritage 1999).[2] However, it also includes the discovery of major new monuments such as the Beckhampton Avenue (Fig. 5) during large-scale excavation projects (Gillings and Pollard 2004).

In Avebury there is a strong link between ongoing archaeological investigations and the management

Figure 4   Avebury: Visitor erosion along the top of the Henge bank.

[2] The National Mapping Programme is long-term project started in the 1980s and run by the English Heritage Aerial Survey Department. It aims to enhance our understanding of the nation's landscape by using aerial photographs and it has already covered around a third of the country.

Figure 5   A buried sarsen in the lost Beckhampton Avenue under excavation in 2003.

of the WHS. Work began in 1996 on the development of a WHS Research Agenda for the site and this was published in 2001. It was the first of its kind for a WHS. The Research Agenda set out to assess our current state of knowledge for all periods in the past and to identify future research priorities (see paper in this volume by Batchelor). The Agenda was closely linked to the first WHS management plan and there are current plans to revise the document in the light of recent discoveries.

STRENGTHS AND WEAKNESSES IN THE MANAGEMENT OF THE AVEBURY WHS

The next part of the paper focuses on an overall analysis of the strengths and weaknesses of the Avebury WHS, and the successes and failures in the management of the site. It is a difficult and subjective exercise, which does not attempt any comparative analysis with other sites because of the marked differences between World Heritage Sites.

Certainly one of the strengths of Avebury as a visitor attraction is the open and unrestricted access to almost all the monuments that are free of charge; the exception is Silbury Hill, which is not open to public access. The diverse range of archaeological and historic features to experience at the site is also an attraction to a wide range of visitors, as is the re-use of some of the historic buildings, such as the Barn Gallery Exhibition, for visitor use. The existence of a museum at the heart of site displaying artefacts from the excavations within the WHS is unique. The main strength, however, is the surviving prehistoric monumental landscape architecture with its intrinsic educational and research values.

Any visitor to Avebury will not have failed to observe that main road, which splits the Henge monument in two, is a major detraction. The road, traffic and the site's vulnerability to parking congestion are all drawbacks to visitors to the site and contribute to the potential for conflict between the

villagers and tourists. It has been recognised since the 1990s that visitor numbers have exceeded sustainable levels. The site is vulnerable to erosion and its open access means it has low potential for generating enough income to deal with all of the conservation requirements. The involvement of multiple agencies in the management of the site can be seen as a weakness rather than a strength here as it has lead to a wide sense of ownership of the site but not necessarily to a widespread sense of responsibility.

Since Avebury was inscribed as a WHS in 1986, together with Stonehenge, there has been mixed success in the implementation of the various management objectives and measures.

The development of the both management plans (English Heritage 1998 and 2005) has clearly succeeded in building consensus and partnerships and the plans have been generally well received. The publication of the archaeological research agenda (Chadburn and Pomeroy-Kellinger 2001) as the first of its kind has helped to co-ordinate research and has contributed to the new discoveries. A recent questionnaire issued by the Avebury WHS Officer to canvass views on the Research Agenda generated positive responses in terms of the usefulness of the document especially in helping to gain funding for targeted research. Other successes include the development of a special Countryside Stewardship project set up in 2001 to permit the payment of enhanced sums to farmers within the WHS for taking archaeological sites out of arable cultivation.[3] This resulted in the conversion of 5% of the land within the WHS to grassland within a five year period. This and other small-scale partnership projects (such as improving the access to and setting of West Kennet Long Barrow in 2002–3) have succeeded in make a real difference to the preservation and enhancement of the monuments. In terms of interpretation, the successful conversion of the Barn into an exhibition about the Avebury landscape has greatly enhanced the visitor experience of the WHS.

There has been much less success in tackling some of the fundamental issues facing Avebury, such as securing long-term funding for major partnership projects and gaining commitments to this from the local authorities. Similarly, there has been little progress made on tackling either the ongoing problems of erosion on the Henge, or the impact of the roads, traffic and parking congestion on the village.

The priorities for the future management of this unique WHS should be firstly focus on the securing of long-term funding for its preservation. The continuous monitoring of the state of conservation of the monuments together with an assessment of sustainable visitor numbers should be a priority for the site managers. In addition, the recommendations made

---

[3] Countryside Stewardship (CSS) was a 10-year agri-environmental scheme funded and operated by the Department for Environment, Food and Rural Affairs (DEFRA). Since 2005 it has been replaced by a similar but two-tier scheme, the Environmental Stewardship Scheme.

for the revision to the WHS boundaries should be forwarded to UNESCO for endorsement as soon as possible by the DCMS.

Bibliography

Chadburn, A, and Pomeroy –Kellinger, M, (eds) 2001 *Archaeological Research Agenda for the Avebury World Heritage Site*, Avebury Archaeological Research Group, Trust for Wessex Archaeology/ English Heritage

English Heritage, 1998 *Avebury World Heritage Site Management Plan*

English Heritage, 1999 *National Mapping Programme. The Avebury WHS Mapping Project*

English Heritage, 2005 *Avebury World Heritage Site Management Plan*

Gillings, M, and Pollard, J, 2004 *Avebury*, London, Duckworth

Implementing a World Heritage Site Management Plan – an Outline of Recent Projects at Stonehenge

Isabelle Bedu

INTRODUCTION

Visited by 800,000 people a year, Stonehenge (3000–1600 BC) is the most famous prehistoric monument in the world, but also one of the least understood and less well presented to the public. Today, Stonehenge is sandwiched between two roads and the sight and noise of traffic are omnipresent during the visit. The facilities are too small for the number of visitors and there is no space for any exhibition on site. The surrounding prehistoric monuments, which are also of international significance and an integral part of the World Heritage Site (WHS) designation, are still largely unknown to the public.

This paper outlines the major changes proposed in the WHS Management Plan to improve the setting of Stonehenge, enhance the understanding of the whole landscape, and improve the conservation of its many prehistoric monuments. After describing the significance of Stonehenge and its surrounding monuments, it outlines the vision in the WHS Management Plan, emphasising the importance of partnership. Finally, it provides an update on the projects underway to make the vision reality.

SIGNIFICANCE OF THE STONEHENGE WORLD HERITAGE SITE

A good understanding of what is special about a cultural or natural site is essential to ensure its adequate conservation, management and presentation to the public.

The Stonehenge and Avebury World Heritage Site

'Stonehenge, Avebury and associated sites' were inscribed as a single World Heritage Site in 1986 for their outstanding prehistoric monuments. Stonehenge is located 40 km south of Avebury.[1]

A summary description of the Stonehenge and Avebury World Heritage Site can be found in the recent UNESCO Periodic Report (Bedu and Pomeroy-Kellinger 2005):

> Stonehenge and Avebury, in Wiltshire, are the two most important prehistoric monuments in Britain. Stonehenge is the most sophisticated stone circle in the world and Avebury is the largest. Both were built and used in the

Neolithic and early Bronze-Age, probably for ceremonial activities although their exact function is still unknown. With the outstanding ritual and funerary monuments surrounding them, they each form a unique landscape and an incomparable testimony to prehistoric times.

Separate WHS Management Plans were produced for Avebury (English Heritage 1998) and Stonehenge (Chris Blandford Associates 2000). In both cases, the first part of the plan details the significance of the site, in accordance with international conservation guidelines such as the Burra Charter and UK best practice for management and conservation plans (Clark 1999 and 2001, Countryside Commission 1998).

Assessment of significance of the Stonehenge World Heritage Site (Fig. 1)

The World Heritage Site boundary at Stonehenge covers a large area totalling 2,600 hectares, and includes 784 archaeological features, 416 of which are protected as Scheduled Monuments. Many people know about Stonehenge but very few are aware of the wealth of surrounding prehistoric features. Stonehenge itself, although iconic, is far from being well understood and its function remains a mystery. When assessing its significance, it is also important to understand what makes it so special amongst the hundreds of stone circles in Europe.

The significance of the Stonehenge World Heritage Site can be considered from four angles: (1) Stonehenge itself, as one of the most sophisticated prehistoric monuments in the world; (2) Stonehenge as a sacred place providing a link with our ancestors; (3) the other outstanding prehistoric monuments from the Neolithic to the early Bronze Age within the WHS; (4) the World Heritage Site as a living landscape supporting a range of varied interests.

1 Stonehenge – the sophisticated structure

Stonehenge was built and used by prehistoric people between 3000 and 1600 BC, in the late Neolithic and Early Bronze-Age periods. Its construction was extremely complex and the details are still not fully understood, but it was built in several phases:

- 1st phase – Earthen monument – circular bank and ditch (about 3000 BC).
- 2nd phase – Timber monument and alignment on solstice sunrise.

---

[1] For more information on Avebury, see article by Melanie Pomeroy-Kellinger in this publication and www.kennet.gov.uk/aveburywhs.

33

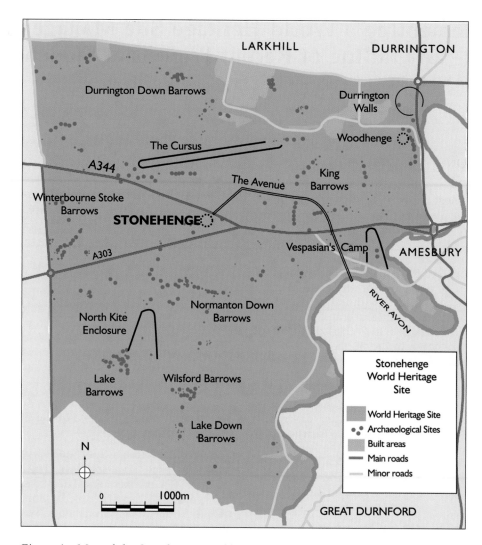

Figure 1   Map of the Stonehenge World Heritage Site (2003 © English Heritage).

- 3rd phase – Stone monument – 'blue' stones (2500 BC) and Sarsen circle and Horseshoe after successive re-arrangements (2400 to 1600 BC) – abandoned after 1600 BC.

The Stonehenge Avenue, the largest Trilithon and the so-called 'altar' stone at its base were built on the line of the midsummer sunrise (although some archaeologists now suggest that the winter solstice was more significant). Such alignments are common at other prehistoric sites (for instance at Newgrange, where the end of the burial chamber is lit by the rising sun on the winter solstice).

Although there are hundreds of stone circles in Europe, Stonehenge is unparalleled. What makes it truly unique is the engineering feat of the Sarsen circle, with its lintels and sophisticated mortice-and-tenon joints, its perfect geometry with circular and horizontal alignments, and its squared, shaped stones (Fig. 2). The provenance of the stones, with a combination of blue stones from the Preseli Mountain in Wales (385 km distant) and Sarsen stones from the Marlborough Downs (40 km away),

is also unusual. Finally, the sheer size of the Sarsen stones (40 tonnes for the largest) is worth a mention. Stonehenge is a monumental achievement of a wealthy and powerful society. It is arguably the most sophisticated stone circle in the world.

2   Stonehenge – a sacred site

An intrinsic quality of Stonehenge is its sacred character. The exact function of Stonehenge remains a mystery. Archaeological surveys have shown that it is most probably a sacred site where ceremonial activities would have taken place, although no specific artefacts have been found, unlike sites like the megalithic temples of Malta which have produced statuettes of a mother goddess. The only hard facts that indicate how it may have been used are the cremation burials around the earthen bank in its earlier phase, the alignment on the midsummer sunrise, and the grand architecture of the stone circle. Despite centuries of conjecture and archaeological research, we can still only propose educated guesses: a temple to the sun possibly linked to

Figure 2 Stonehenge: Unparalleled in its architectural quality and as a feat of engineering (James O. Davies 2004 © English Heritage).

fertility and successful harvests, a sacred site to celebrate the dead, an astronomical observatory to map the movements of the sun and the moon.

The stone circle still provides a link with our ancestors and retains a sense of sacred for many. It is an international icon, and it was recently short-listed for the new Seven Wonders of the World, an international web poll running in 2005–2007. Its universal appeal is also illustrated by the high proportion of foreign visitors (about 50% of the total).

Although the memory of its original use has been lost, some celebrations still take place at Stonehenge today. Of course, these are modern inventions following the fashions of the time, but they show the depth of attraction of Stonehenge (Chippindale 2004).

The alignment on the sunrise has led to solstice celebrations, on a small scale in the 19th century and with a different twist in the 1970s, when Stonehenge became the site of a huge gathering for an alternative music festival. This led to severe problems and for 15 years an exclusion zone was created during the solstice period. Since 2000, English Heritage has reopened the stone circle for the solstice and it is now a peaceful event, which attracted 20,000 people on 21 June 2005.

The stone circle has also been used for druidic ceremonies, which were first recorded in the early 20th century. This association between Stonehenge and the druids is mainly due to the writings of the

18th-century antiquarian William Stukeley, who believed that Stonehenge was a temple built by the druids (Chippindale 2004, chapters 4–5).

3 Stonehenge in context

Stonehenge is surrounded by a dense concentration of archaeological remains mainly from the Neolithic and Bronze Age, including hundreds of burial mounds, some ancient settlements and field systems, and other distinctive monuments such as the Avenue, the Cursus, Woodhenge and Durrington Walls.[2]

The Avenue is a ceremonial route aligned on the Solstice sunrise, or possibly the sunset, and formed the main entrance into Stonehenge. It is 3 km long and 30 metres wide, and links Stonehenge to the river Avon (Fig. 3). It was in use between 2500 and 1700 BC, at the time of the construction of the stone circle. It is now cut by the A344 which passes only metres from the Heel Stone, one of the pair of stones marking the sun alignment.

The Cursus is another huge monument made of earth. Dating from about 3100 BC (Neolithic), it precedes the first phase of Stonehenge. It is 2.8 km long and 90 metres wide, with a long barrow at the eastern end and a round barrow at the western end. It is one of class of monuments whose function remains a mystery.

Durrington Walls is a late Neolithic enclosure in use between 3100 and 2500 BC. It is the largest henge in Europe (500 metres in diameter). It was similar to the Avebury henge, which is much better preserved, but the banks and ditch of Durrington Walls have been much eroded by time. Excavations inside the enclosure in 1967 revealed two circular timber structures and huge quantities of bones and pottery, suggesting that feasting may have taken place there. In 2005, a new research project found evidence of a short avenue linking Durrington Walls to the river Avon and of small Neolithic houses located just outside the bank.

Near Durrington Walls, Woodhenge is contemporary to the stone circle (2300–2000 BC). It was found by aerial photography, which revealed 6 rings of wooden posts. It is not clear whether the posts would have supported a roof or whether they were free standing. Some archaeologists interpret them as totem poles for the dead. In the middle of the circle, a child with a split skull is buried. As is the case for Stonehenge, the function of these ceremonial monuments remains unclear.

The rest of the landscape around Stonehenge is dotted with prehistoric burial mounds, and could be likened to a huge cemetery. The most prominent barrow cemeteries are the Winterbourne Stoke Barrows,

---

[2] For more details about the stone circle and the surrounding monuments see the recently revised guidebook published by English Heritage (Richards 2005), and also Chippindale 2004 and Souden 1997. A virtual tour of the many monuments making up the Stonehenge World Heritage Site is available on www.english-heritage.org.uk/stonehenge.

Figure 3 Stonehenge and its Avenue: a ceremonial route leading into the stone circle, and now cut by the A344 (NMR © English Heritage).

King Barrows and Normanton Down Barrows (Fig. 4 below). There are 346 Bronze Age round barrows, many of them flattened by ploughing, and ten Neolithic long barrows within the boundaries of the World Heritage Site. Typical objects found in these barrows would include pottery and flint arrowheads, but Bush Barrow on Normanton Down contained a finely worked gold lozenge plate, a mace, and several bronze daggers, indicating power and wealth. These artefacts are on display in the Devizes and Salisbury museums.

4 Stonehenge World Heritage Site – a living landscape

The Stonehenge World Heritage Site supports a farming community and private residential housing in Larkhill, Durrington, Amesbury and the Woodford Valley. It is criss-crossed by rights of way used by local walkers and cyclists.

Nature conservation is also one of the values of the World Heritage Site. Its chalk grassland is important in its own right and as a habitat for wild flowers, birds and insects. Many protected birds can be found

in this area, and the RSPB has recently created a stone-curlew reserve in the southern part of the World Heritage Site.

Finally, the economic importance of the site must be mentioned. Stonehenge is the gateway to the south-west of England and, as one of the most visited cultural sites in the country, it plays a major role in the regional and national economy.

THE VISION OF THE WORLD HERITAGE SITE MANAGEMENT PLAN

This section outlines the major changes planned to improve the setting of Stonehenge and enhance the visitor experience, and which aim to protect and enhance the outstanding and universal value of the site. It emphasises in particular the holistic approach of the Management Plan, seeking to balance different interests, and the importance of partnership to make the vision reality.

Ownership and management context

The ownership of the World Heritage Site is shared between English Heritage, the National Trust, the Ministry of Defence, six large farms, and many private residences. English Heritage owns Stonehenge and Woodhenge. The National Trust owns most of the landscape visible from Stonehenge, including the Avenue, the Cursus, King Barrows, Winterbourne Stoke Barrows, and Durrington Walls.

English Heritage is the government's agency for the protection of cultural heritage, and the National Trust is an independent charity set up in 1895 to protect historic houses and beautiful landscapes. Sites within the WHS are protected by a wide range of statutory and non-statutory designations, and include scheduled monuments, listed buildings, and conservation areas. Some of the area is also safeguarded as National Trust inalienable land, which cannot be sold by the Trust or be subjected to compulsory purchase, and is therefore protected forever.

Key issues

Today Stonehenge suffers from a number of problems, identified in the WHS Management Plan.

The setting of this ancient monument is marred by two roads (Fig. 5), one of them passing only metres away from the Heel Stone (Fig. 3). The increase in traffic on the A303 has meant that, Stonehenge has also become a black-spot for congestion and accidents. The car park, the visitor facilities and the fence separating English Heritage land from the road also add to these modern intrusions. The first impressions on arrival are dominated by modern clutter, and the dignity and sense of sacred are somewhat lost as a result.

The visitor facilities, built in 1968 as temporary structures, are now inadequate for the number of visitors and do not meet the standards expected at a World Heritage Site. There is congestion in the car

Figure 4   Normanton Down Barrows: since this area reverted to pasture in 2003, these prehistoric burial mounds are no longer isolated islands in a sea of crops (NMR 15041–06 © English Heritage).

park on peak days, huge queues at the ticket office and visitors have to battle their way into the tiny shop. There is no space for any panels explaining the stone circle and the surrounding monuments, and the interpretation relies almost entirely on the audio-tour included in the entrance fee. There is a small take-away café struggling to cope with the demand on busy days, without any indoor sitting area for visitors. Because the facilities are so close to Stonehenge and located in such an archaeologically sensitive area, it would be unacceptable to upgrade or extend them in situ.

The surrounding prehistoric monuments, which are also of international significance and an integral part of the WHS designation, are still largely unknown to the public and access to them is not obvious. Many of the monuments are still under arable agriculture and suffer from plough damage while others suffer from a lack of management leading to scrub encroachment and damage from burrowing animals.

Some of these issues were first recognised 30 years ago in 1975 when the first meeting about the roads took place. In 1984, a Stonehenge Study Group was set up to improve the visitor experience and reduce the negative impact of the neighbouring roads on the site. During the following years, several schemes were proposed for Stonehenge. Over 50 alternative routes were considered for the A303, as well as a

long, bored tunnel and a short tunnel. Re-routing of the A303 was rejected because of its negative impacts and the tunnels were discarded because of their cost. The following locations for a new visitor centre were considered and rejected following extensive consultation: Larkhill, Countess Farm, Fargo North.[3] But there was no obvious solution and no progress was made. In 1993, the House of Commons Public Accounts Committee described the situation at Stonehenge as 'a national disgrace'. Today, the situation is unchanged if not worse as annual visitor numbers have increased to around 800,000 in 2000.

Since the first fence and entrance fee were introduced at Stonehenge in 1901, it has been necessary to adapt the facilities to the growing numbers of visitors on several occasions.[4] It is now a matter of urgency to extend and improve the existing facilities.

The Stonehenge World Heritage Site Management Plan

Given the multiple ownership of the World Heritage Site, the difficulty of the issues and the wide appeal

---

[3] A summary of the various road and visitor centre schemes can be found at the beginning of Chris Blandford Associates 1998.
[4] For a historical account, see Chippindale 2004. For a visual account, see Richards 2004.

of Stonehenge, producing a Management Plan for the whole site was no easy task. The process, led by consultants, took two years and involved consultation with a wide range of interested parties. The Stonehenge WHS Management Plan was published in 2000 by English Heritage and endorsed by the key stakeholders (Chris Blandford Associates 2000).

The Management Plan provides a strategy for the future of the whole World Heritage Site. It is a framework for the holistic and sustainable management of the site. It seeks to balance the primary aim of protecting the archaeological landscape for future generations, with other interests such as visitor access, farming, and nature conservation.

Based on a detailed assessment of the significance of the site and of the key management issues, the Management Plan outlines objectives for the short, medium and long term. It includes a detailed action plan with target dates and clear responsibilities. It follows the same format as the Avebury Management Plan.

The vision for the future of Stonehenge

Combining conservation and access objectives, the WHS Management Plan recommends major changes for the future, seeking not only to protect but also to enhance the outstanding universal value of the site. Its long-term objectives include:

• Removing traffic and modern intrusions from the vicinity of Stonehenge,
• Extending the grass setting around Stonehenge and reuniting the stone circle with its neighbouring monuments,
• Building a new world-class visitor centre with exhibitions and education facilities, to be located just outside the World Heritage Site,
• Improving access to and enjoyment of the many monuments surrounding Stonehenge.

The Management Plan envisages a core area of permanent grassland around Stonehenge, free of traffic and modern intrusions, and managed for open access on foot. A new world- class visitor centre would be built outside the WHS so that the existing facilities could be removed. Visitors would have a choice of drop off points to discover the other monuments of the WHS, and make the final approach to Stonehenge on foot. Archaeological sites would be protected from plough damage with the land reverting to pasture. This would also improve the ecological value of the site. Mixed farming would continue in the wider landscape, where access would be possible using the existing public rights of way and potential new routes. Research and educational activities would be encouraged to improve the understanding of the World Heritage Site.

Implementation of the World Heritage Site Management Plan

To implement the plan, it was recommended that a small executive group and a larger advisory group

be put in place and a World Heritage Site Coordinator be appointed.

The Stonehenge WHS Committee is the executive group, composed of the key stakeholders. It meets quarterly to receive reports on projects underway, agree priorities and ensure co-ordination between the Stonehenge partners. It is composed of the landowners (English Heritage, the National Trust, Ministry of Defence, and farmers), the planning authorities (district and county), representatives of the local community, and national bodies (Ministry for Culture, ICOMOS UK, Highways Agency, English Nature).

The WHS Advisory Forum is composed of 45 organisations and individuals who took part in the preparation of the Management Plan. It meets once year for an annual review of the implementation of the Plan and to provide feedback on projects. Small working groups have also been put in place for specific projects. A WHS Co-ordinator was recruited in 2001 in order to facilitate the delivery of the Management Plan.

The WHS Management Plan sets out an ambitious vision, and its implementation requires the support and participation of many stakeholders and partners involved in Stonehenge. The importance of partnership to make the vision reality can not be over emphasised.

To resolve the issue of the roads and inadequate visitor facilities, the following projects are under consideration, aiming at completion within the next 10 years:

• The main road (A303) will be hidden from view of Stonehenge in a bored tunnel – led by the Highways Agency.
• The local road (A344) will be closed and grassed over to reunite Stonehenge and the Avenue – Highways Agency, English Heritage, Wiltshire County Council.
• A new visitor centre will be built in Amesbury, just outside the World Heritage Site, with exhibition space, education facilities, adequate parking and better links with public transport – led by English Heritage.
• The present car park and visitor facilities near the Stones will be replaced by a small underground area with toilets and first aid – English Heritage.

Several projects, delivering other key objectives of the WHS Management Plan, have already been completed since 2000:

Conservation and research

• In 2001, the National Trust produced a Land Use Plan outlining priorities for farming, conservation, wildlife and public access.
• Since 2002, in order to stop plough damage, the Ministry for Agriculture (DEFRA) has been providing special grants to farmers for the conversion of arable fields to pasture in archaeologically sensitive areas.

- A survey was carried out (Wessex Archaeology 2003) to assess the condition of over 650 archaeological features in the WHS, identifying key threats and making recommendations to improve their conservation.
- A set of WHS monitoring indicators for Stonehenge and Avebury was produced in 2003
- A Stonehenge Archaeological Research Framework was published in 2005, setting out priorities for future research in the World Heritage Site (see Batchelor this volume).

Access, interpretation and education

- An education project aimed at local primary schools was developed in 2003, focused on Stonehenge, Avebury and World Heritage Sites (see Bunyard this volume).
- New signposts indicating the distance to the prehistoric monuments were installed in 2004 to help people discover the wider Stonehenge landscape.
- An interactive map of the Stonehenge landscape went live on the English Heritage website in 2004, offering a virtual tour of the key prehistoric monuments of the WHS, including those without physical access (www.english-heritage.org.uk/ stonehengeinteractivemap).
- A team of volunteers was put in place by the National Trust in 2004, delivering amongst other activities, a Stonehenge summer school, an oral history project, and guided tours.

Many other projects have been completed or started since the publication of the Management Plan in 2000, and a full review is available from the WHS Co-ordinator.

UPDATE ON PROJECTS

This section provides an update on key projects delivering the vision of the World Heritage Site Management Plan.

Free Stonehenge from traffic

After nearly 30 years trying to find a solution to the road problem at Stonehenge, a breakthrough finally came in 1998, when the Government made a commitment to fund a 2 km cut and cover tunnel for Stonehenge. After the first surveys and design proposals, it was decided in 2002 to opt for a 2.1 km bored tunnel which was included in the road programme. The A303 road scheme also included a flyover at the Amesbury roundabout, dualling of the A303 in the WHS, an improved junction at Long Barrow Crossroad and a bypass of the village of Winterbourne Stoke outside the WHS.

Because of the sensitivity of the area, the Highways Agency conducted the project as an 'exemplary environmental scheme', recruiting a contractor early on and ensuring that the impacts of construction would be assessed as thoroughly as the final impacts. Much consultation took place on the route,

and the proposed works managed to avoid any direct impact on any scheduled monuments, which is quite remarkable given the density of archaeological features.

The details of the proposed road scheme (Environmental Impact Assessment and Draft Orders) were published in 2003 and scrutinised during a Public Inquiry which took place from February till May 2004. The Inspector concluded in favour of the scheme, recognising some detrimental effect on the setting of some monuments, but judging that overall the benefits of the scheme largely outweighed any negative impacts. But in July 2005, the government announced a review of the options for the A303 because of increased costs.

The options currently being considered include the 2.1 km bored tunnel, a 2 km cut and cover tunnel, 2 by passes going North and South of Stonehenge through the WHS, and a 'partial solution' closing the A344 but leaving the A303 as it is. This review includes a 3-month public consultation before a decision by Ministers in the summer 2006. The future of the proposed Stonehenge tunnel is therefore currently uncertain.

Build a world-class visitor centre

This project, led by English Heritage, involves the construction of a new visitor centre located outside the WHS, access through the landscape to Stonehenge using a land train with several drop off points, and removal of the existing car park and facilities.

Using interactive and audio-visual techniques, the visitor centre would tell the story of Stonehenge and the wider landscape. It would include educational facilities, a larger shop and an indoor café. It would also benefit from ample parking and good links with public transport, being located in Amesbury near Countess Roundabout. A land train would take visitors to a series of drop off points, providing access to Woodhenge, Durrington Walls, King Barrows and the Cursus, before a final stop some 20 minutes walk away from Stonehenge. Visitors would then approach Stonehenge on foot in a landscape free of any modern intrusions. The existing car park and buildings would be removed and grassed over, retaining only minimal underground facilities (toilets, sitting, shelter and staff area).

This is an exemplary project combining access and conservation objectives. It seeks to improve the setting of Stonehenge and to give visitors a better appreciation of the whole World Heritage Site. It is hoped that the length of the visit would increase to 2 to 3 hours, as opposed to the present 45 minutes.

In 2000, English Heritage acquired the site for the proposed visitor centre. In 2001, a bid was submitted to the Heritage Lottery Fund and the architects Denton Corker Marshall were chosen after an international competition. The design proposals, consultation on the access proposals from the visitor centre to Stonehenge, and the Environmental Impact Assessment were developed in 2002–4. The planning

Figure 5   Stonehenge: sandwiched between the A303 and the A344 (Chris Newton © English Heritage).

application submitted in September 2004 was refused by Salisbury District Council in July 2005 because of the impact of the land train and the uncertainty over access from the A303. English Heritage decided to appeal in November 2005. The future of the visitor centre is therefore also uncertain at present.[5]

Grass restoration

Since 2002, in order to stop plough damage to prehistoric monuments, the Ministry of Agriculture (DEFRA) has been providing special grants to farmers for the conversion of arable fields to pasture (Fig. 5). A rate 50% higher than the norm was negotiated for the Stonehenge and Avebury World Heritage Site. This exemplary partnership between DEFRA, English Heritage, the National Trust and the WHS farmers provides benefits for archaeological sites, nature conservation and also access, as the National Trust has pledged to provide open access to its land where it has reverted to grass.

This project proved very successful: in 2005, 340 hectares were signed up to return to pasture at Stonehenge, protecting 75 ancient monuments (Fig. 6). This represents about 20% of the land which was under cultivation at the beginning of the scheme. Most of the priorities for grass restoration identified in 2002 have been covered by the agreements signed to date.

CONCLUSION

The Stonehenge WHS Management Plan provides an ambitious vision for the future which was endorsed by all the stakeholders. This in itself is a remarkable achievement. But passing from a strategic plan to action on the ground is no easy task as shown by Jon Kohl in a recent article (Kohl 2005). At Stonehenge, there has been good progress in some areas, and some disappointments in other areas.

The grass restoration scheme was extremely successful despite starting just after the foot and mouth crisis. Its success was partly due to the enticing rate negotiated for the World Heritage Site and partly to the effective partnership working closely together to make it happen. On the other hand, the challenge of reuniting Stonehenge with its

---

[5] Further information on the road and visitor centre projects can be found on www.thestonehengeproject.org.

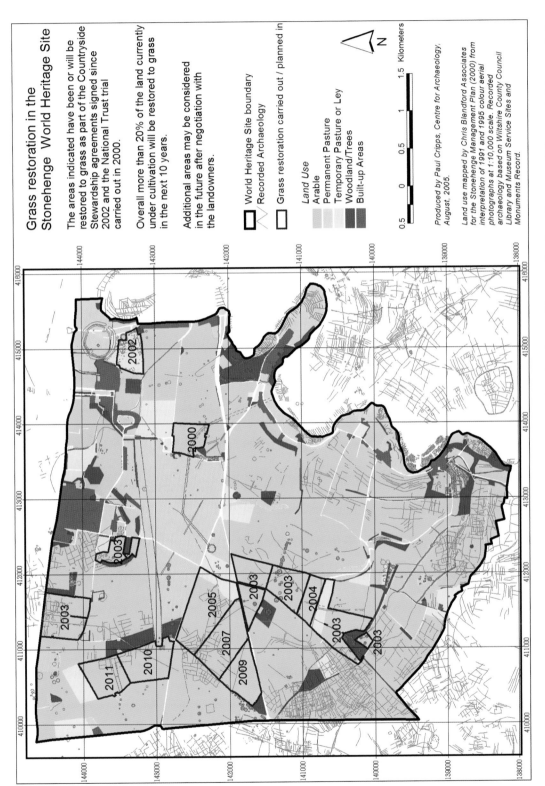

Figure 6 Map of grass restoration in the Stonehenge World Heritage Site, showing arable areas that have been or will be reverted to grass between 2002 and 2012 (2005 © English Heritage).

landscape is still unresolved after decades of efforts. It is now time to ensure that the changes recommended in the Management Plan happen on the ground.

Effective partnership, keeping all interested parties on board, is essential. And sometimes, as in the case of the Stonehenge tunnel, funding is indeed an issue.

Bibliography

Australia ICOMOS, 1999, *Burra Charter*

Bedu, I, 2005 A special grant scheme for World Heritage Site farmers at Stonehenge and Avebury, *Conservation Bulletin*, Issue **50** Autumn 2005, 26–27

Bedu, I, and Pomeroy-Kellinger, M, 2005 *Stonehenge and Avebury World Heritage Site Periodic Report*, English Heritage

Cathersides, A, 2001 Stonehenge – Restoration of grassland setting, *Conservation Bulletin*, Issue **40** March 2001, 34–36

Chippindale, C 2004 *Stonehenge Complete*, London, Thames and Hudson (esp. chapters 4 and 5 on Stonehenge and the Druids)

Chris Blandford Associates 1998 *Stonehenge World Heritage Site Management Plan Project – Framework for Discussion*, English Heritage

Chris Blandford Associates, 2000 *Stonehenge World Heritage Site Management Plan*, English Heritage

Clark, K, 1999 *Conservation Plans in Action: proceedings of the Oxford conference*, London: English Heritage

Clark, K, 2001 *Informed Conservation: understanding historic buildings and their landscapes for conservation*, London: English Heritage

Countryside Commission, 1998 *Site management Planning – A Guide*

English Heritage, 1998 *Avebury World Heritage Site Management Plan*

English Heritage, 2005a *Stonehenge World Heritage Site: An Archaeological Research Framework*

English Heritage, 2005b *Avebury World Heritage Site Management Plan*

Kohl, J, 2005 Converting unseen and unexpected barriers to park plan implementation into manageable and expected challenges, *Parks, the International Journal for Protected Area Managers* (IUCN) vol. **15** (**1**), 45–57

Richards, J, 2004 *Stonehenge – A history in photographs*, English Heritage

Richards, J, 2005*Stonehenge Guidebook*, English Heritage

Souden, D, 1997 *Stonehenge – Mysteries of the Stones and Landscape*, English Heritage

Wessex Archaeology 2003, *Condition survey and management recommendations for archaeological sites within the Stonehenge World Heritage Site*, English Heritage

The Stonehenge and Avebury World Heritage Site Education Project

Margaret Bunyard

INTRODUCTION

How can you introduce a new generation of school children to their country's prehistoric heritage when the subject is not part of the National Curriculum? How can you convince people that there is far more to interest them at Stonehenge and Avebury than the standing stones alone? What can be done to make the designation 'World Heritage Site' meaningful to the people who live near one, and how can teachers who have never studied archaeology gain enough background information to use its findings with confidence in their teaching?

These were the ambitious challenges the Stonehenge and Avebury WHS (World Heritage Site) Project was designed to meet. The stone circles at Avebury and Stonehenge date respectively to the Neolithic and Early Bronze Age in Britain. Both are designated World Heritage Sites.

PLANNING AND PROBLEMS

The project was the outcome of a partnership between education staff at English Heritage and Wessex Archaeology, World Heritage Site Officers at Stonehenge and Avebury, Salisbury Museum and local primary schools. In the second year, when the main focus was on Avebury, the project also benefited from the support of the National Trust. Wessex Archaeology is an archaeological practice, but was established as a charity with the remit to encourage people's interest and awareness of their past. As the company is based near Stonehenge and has undertaken fieldwork there over many years, it was keen to become involved.

In outline, the plan was first to set up a steering group which would design a six-week scheme of work, with a site visit as the focal point, and test it with one or more pilot schools. Assuming a good outcome, the steering group would organise and run a teacher–training day so that the ideas could be examined and discussed by a group of interested teachers. Finally, based on the work with children and the views of teachers, the material and experience would be used to produce a scheme of work for studying prehistory at primary school level in a format that would be familiar to teachers across the country. To do this, the scheme of work would be drawn up in line with those on the Qualifications and Curriculum Authority website. These serve as accepted guidelines and models of good practice and are widely used for teaching history at primary school level.

The teacher–training day was seen as an essential part in the whole process, allowing us to discuss our project and test our ideas with a critical audience. Although we would be working with teachers and their pupils throughout the project, we would need to be sure that activities that worked for them would be suitable for other schools and other groups of children.

This apparently straightforward plan was more of a challenge than it might seem. Not only are archaeology and prehistory barely visible within the school curriculum, but learning about heritage sites and visiting heritage site are activities seldom undertaken in British schools. The situation ought not to be like this. In 2001 the government made the welcome statement that it 'looks to a future in which the full potential of the historic environment as a learning resource is realised' (English Heritage 2001, 9). 'Out of school learning' is a buzz phrase at the moment (2006). However, there is no requirement in the National Curriculum to make this a reality: rather there are many difficulties in the way of schools attempting it; timetabling, the cost of travel and entrance fees, the obvious need for risk assessments and the extra staffing required to take children on a school trip. It is, moreover, unlikely that teachers will, without support and encouragement, include World Heritage Sites in their planning since there is nothing in the curricula for England, Wales or Ireland that develops a concern for the past in the form of a physical heritage to be preserved for future generations (Henson, in Henson, Stone and Corbishley, 2004, 25).

The academic year was already underway when the first planning meeting was held in November 2003 and it rapidly became clear that it was not going to be easy to find a school willing to commit itself to piloting a project when the work had not already been built into their forward planning. However, time was short, the English Heritage Regional Education Officer was soon to be seconded to a different post, and the project had to be moved forward at speed or else abandoned or postponed for more than a year.

IMPLEMENTATION – STONEHENGE PILOT PROJECT

We needed to pilot the project first at Stonehenge, so it was a relief when finally, in March 2004, the Headteacher of Amesbury Junior School agreed to let a probationary teacher, then in her first year of teaching, join us with her year five class (nine and ten year olds). It was agreed that members of the team would work in the classroom for four consecutive afternoons before leading an all day visit to the site, later returning to school for two further afternoons of follow-up work.

Planning and preparation

Planning a programme of six weeks' work for children with no background knowledge of a historic period is a task with which teachers are all familiar. But to do this for a prehistoric period is more of a challenge. There are some excellent handbooks for teachers, produced by English Heritage, some of which have been in circulation for many years. These give good ideas for activities and useful explanations and background reading for teachers. It is the lack of resources for children, which presents the biggest problem. Archaeologists are not writing books which are accessible and appealing to a young audience! There are very few designed to inform young children about the distant past, and fewer still that are exciting. Web resources are improving and the number of good ones growing. More and more schools have white–boards in the classroom and can teach a lesson based on internet materials to the whole class, but there are not enough good books to support this work.

The first sessions set the scene and helped the children understand what is meant by the term World Heritage Site. They listened to a presentation by the WHS Officer for Stonehenge and played a game which matched pictures of the sites to their locations on a world map.

Exciting places capture the attention, but the need for preservation and conservation is not immediately obvious to young children, so they were encouraged to think about what makes something valuable and worth looking after. They were shown an old suitcase containing a variety of ephemera: an old photograph, a baby's shoe, a broken bracelet, a child's drawing etc., and invited to help sort the contents for an imaginary old lady. For each item they needed to decide whether it should be sold, kept for sentimental reasons, given to a museum or thrown away. After much discussion they agreed that things could be precious to different people and for a variety of reasons, and recommended that everything should either be kept or given to a museum. What is true of objects they decided would be true of places too.

The next lessons were focussed on archaeology as a way of finding out about the past. It was important in these sessions to stress the word *evidence* and how archaeologists find out and come to conclusions, since looking at evidence, considering its reliability and drawing conclusions from it is one of the key skills to be developed in the history curriculum's programme of study (Fig. 1).

The children enjoyed sifting through a carefully selected bag of rubbish (empty packets, wrappers

Figure 1 Examining the evidence.

and bills), to draw their own conclusions about the members of the family; their diet, pets, hobbies, the shops they went to and the prices of the things they had bought. This activity led naturally to thinking about the survival of evidence, and the characteristics of the archaeological record. What evidence would be left of them in 1,000 years? They enjoyed drawing pictures of vaguely anatomical skeletons suitably adorned with metal watches, zips and plastic buttons which would give clues about their appearance to archaeologists of the future. After this they were eager to handle real archaeological evidence and to attempt to put the small collection of finds they were given into some chronological order.

This work prepared them to consider the value and limitations of archaeological evidence and to differentiate between what can be proven and what is surmised.

By now the Amesbury children were ready to find out more about the Bronze Age, Stonehenge and its landscape. But ideas on chronology and the passage of time are hard for children to grasp. So to get an idea of how long ago the period is, they unrolled a toilet roll with each sheet representing ten years. Their lives were therefore contained within that first piece of paper, and since one roll was not enough to go back as far as the Bronze Age, the message about its antiquity was clear enough.

Helping them learn about this period and place was made much easier and more immediate by the recent discoveries by Wessex Archaeology of the Amesbury Archer and the Boscombe Bowmen. These important finds were discovered within three miles of Stonehenge, and radiocarbon dating puts them between 2400–2200 BC, the Early Bronze Age in Britain. This is the period when the 20 tonne Sarsen stones were brought from the Malborough Downs, and the smaller four tonne Bluestones were transported there from the Preseli Hills in Wales. The children were fascinated by the idea of a night–time rescue dig, by the isotope analysis of the skeletons' teeth and by the collection of finds associated with the burial. They examined photographs of the excavated burial before drawing a picture of how they thought the Archer might have looked, and then saw how a professional artist had interpreted the same evidence.

Site Visit

We had ambitious plans for the site visit based in part on large scale role play projects run with schools by English Heritage and by Hampshire Education Drama Advisers in the 1980s and 1990s. We wanted the children to experience an idea of what it would be like to live in a different time and place. This is more than mere dressing-up. It requires in-depth preparation, with children imagining for themselves a name, a family, home and occupation appropriate for the period they are learning about. Working in role is a tremendously powerful learning tool. It puts the individual child at the centre of the activity and gives each a real reason for doing the research to find out what they need to know to create their in-role identity.

In the 1980s and 1990s, before the arrival of the National Curriculum, it was easier to find time in the school day to spend on the in-depth preparation needed to make this approach to learning successful. It was also much easier to take pupils on a school trip. Coach transport was less expensive, and there was less anxiety about health and safety regulations. However, the situation may be changing. *The Education Out of School Manifesto* was launched by government in February 2005. This aims 'to give all children a wide range of high quality experiences outside the classroom' and promote 'a widespread understanding and acceptance of the unique contribution these experiences make to young lives'. It is to be hoped that this initiative will help increase the number of opportunities for imaginative learning outside of the school building.

Further preparation in school was done with the teacher. The children began to be able to think themselves into the shoes of Bronze Age visitors to Stonehenge. They imagined an alter-ego for themselves, and had an idea of the food they would have eaten, the work they would have done, and the home they would have come from. They researched the design and materials of accessories they would have had and made their own to wear with simple costumes borrowed from English Heritage. Finally, with their teacher, they prepared a 'Bronze Age' meal of vegetable stew, apples, cheese and honey cakes.

The children spent all day on site, in costume and in role for the morning. Mindful of our aim to help them think beyond the Stone Circle, we led them first to the barrows, helping them to think as pilgrims who had travelled a long way to get to this very special place. There they met a re-enactor in the costume of the Amesbury Archer who told them about his journey and his reasons for coming (Fig. 2). They asked him questions about the barrows and processed with him along the Cursus.

A Bronze Age feast was held in the elbow of the Avenue, out of site of the monument so that after lunch the children could process up the slope towards it along the line of the solstice, with the Stones gradually coming into view as they got nearer. This, we hoped, gave them as clear a sense as we could offer them of the feelings of awe and respect that Bronze Age visitors to the site would have felt for the magnificence and scale of the monument.

Once the children had arrived at the Stones, and achieved their 'pilgrimage', the theme of the day changed. We had been asking them to be in costume and stay in role for three hours by now and it was time for a different focus. The WHS Officer wanted to encourage the children to feel involved in

Figure 2   The children were keen to try the deerskin cloak of the 'Amesbury Archer'.

Figure 3   Out of role children record their impressions of the Stonehenge landscape.

the site and to think about its future, and we had another activity to test out on the class (Fig. 3). Now they were to imagine themselves as inspectors for UNESCO, with a checklist of things to look at including signage, access, the shop and the café. By the end of the day they had amassed a wealth of material to work on in school; their experience and feelings about the site, sketches of the monument and its landscape, and reports on the visitor facilities.

Follow-up

Over the next few weeks the children continued their work in school. They painted, drew, wrote poems and sent articles to the local press. They wrote up their reports on the condition of the site and designed visitor facilities for the children who would one day use a new Visitor Centre. Their ideas varied from the predictable sweets and pot noodle machines; to the more thoughtful, a reconstruction of a roundhouse and special audio tours for children; to the imaginative full-sized foam reconstruction of Stonehenge (strangely prescient of a later project by Mike Pitts).

At the end of term, the work was assembled and presented as a small exhibition which was opened at the school, and subsequently moved to the local library, and thence to Salisbury Museum where it stayed for the summer. The Museum generously offered free entrance to the children involved in the project and their parents. This was more than a good will gesture since a straw poll carried out at the beginning of the project showed that many of the children had never before visited a museum.

Evaluation

During the autumn, members of the steering group met to redraft the Scheme of Work in the light of the experience of working with the children, so that it could be offered to a wider audience for comment. That wider audience consisted of the 30 teachers who joined the Teacher Training Day. This was held

at Salisbury Museum, so that participants could familiarise themselves a little with the impressive prehistoric collections. Funding by South West Museums Libraries and Archives Council (SWLAC) helped fund a specialist lecture on Stonehenge and a pack of information and resources for use in schools. It was surprising and enormously cheering to find that so many teachers opted to come on a course about teaching prehistory at primary level when it is not part of the existing curriculum. This surely demonstrates the level of interest particularly amongst schools which are sited reasonably close to heritage sites. As a result of the course, three more schools opted to study Stonehenge in depth the following year, adapting the Scheme of Work to their individual circumstances.

IMPLEMENTATION – AVEBURY PILOT PROJECT

Our plans for the following year, however, also included a second, more ambitious pilot project at Avebury. Here the challenges were different. The period to which we needed to introduce the children was even more remote from their experience. The Neolithic lends itself less easily to recreating the past than the Bronze Age. The risk of misleading children by lack of definite information, and the many ways in which they might misrepresent the period was of concern to some and plans for a site visit in costume and in role were met with some initial anxiety.

Planning and preparation

The number of partners grew. The National Trust, which owns much of the land at Stonehenge but owns and manages the site at Avebury, joined the partners. The local primary school is part of an affiliation of village schools, which share the same topics in order to maximise use of resources. These are village schools, with classes of mixed age and the project rapidly expanded to include 100 children varying in age from five to eleven years old. In addition, the schools came to the subject through a whole curricula approach: the theme for the term's work was to be 'stone' and the prehistory was to fit within that topic.

During the summer term visits to the three schools took the same form as in the previous year and the same subjects were covered, with minor variations in all of them. The site visit would, however be rather different. Firstly, there would be 100 children arriving on site, so more activities would need to be organised. Secondly, the main activity area would be well away from the Stone Circle, in order to allow the sort of freedom of manoeuvre which might be considered distracting for other visitors. Thirdly, the children would retain their prehistoric alter-egos for the whole day.

The children did their own research to give themselves a Neolithic identity in the same way as the children at Amesbury had done, but there were subtle differences. The practical preparation in the schools focussed less on the sort of food to be eaten on site and more on making goods that could be exchanged. Are the children of Amesbury the chefs of tomorrow, and those of Avebury the entrepreneurs? So the 'tribes' which assembled at the Stone Circle and processed to the end of the Avenue, were keen to barter their clay pendants and woollen bracelets and this ensured that the children from the different schools mixed together at the start of the day (Fig. 4).

Site Visit

A number of activities had been organised so that there was enough for everyone to do: the children watched re-enactors knap flint and make arrows, they spun thread, plaited wool, ground wheat and learnt more about the special place they were

visiting. They played a fast-moving game of 'Standing Stones' (a variant of tag invented for the occasion) and then processed back down the Avenue with pipes and drums, to assemble in a circle just inside the monument. Here the charismatic headteacher of Preshute Primary School led the proceedings with a short ceremony to mark the meeting and parting of the assembled tribes of Avebury, and the day was over (Fig. 5).

LESSONS LEARNED

What was learnt from the experiences at Stonehenge and Avebury? First the positive messages:

That working with partners with different perspectives and differing objectives is at least as rewarding as it is challenging. Good communication

Figure 4   The 'Tribes' barter their wares outside the stone circle at Avebury.

Figure 5   Ceremonial dancing at Avebury.

between all parties is clearly vitally important and made easy by email.

Another lesson was that there are schools demonstrably ready and eager to expand the curriculum in order to include a subject as fascinating as prehistory, despite the paucity of resources. It was obvious that the children derived considerable benefit from finding out more about their shared past. Their reactions to the project strongly suggest that they can develop a sense of shared responsibility for and ownership of their heritage site.

The Future

Then the challenge for the future: there are simply not enough resources on hand to support this subject in schools, and market forces suggest it is unlikely that more will become available unless a change in the curriculum drives demand from publishers. There are some worthwhile materials on the internet and English Heritage and Wessex Archaeology have worked together to produce resources which can be down loaded from the Wessex Archaeology website. But more books are needed.

Although these children had a better understanding of the meaning and value of world heritage, not enough use was made of the opportunities and support that exists for linking schools in different parts of the world, for example the UNESCO Asso-

ciated Schools Project Network (ASPnet). We had hoped that the schools near Stonehenge and Avebury would make links with schools abroad, for example in Malta where there are World Heritage Sites from a similar period. This did not happen. It was an add-on that didn't materialise: it should have been a core part of the project from the beginning. In the same way, not enough use was made of the website: it had been our intention that the children would create web pages of their work. There was not enough time.

Was it worth it?

Was it worth it and did we achieve our aims? Evaluation was a key part of the topic, from base level evaluation at the start, through individual activities to a final assessment by teachers and children. There was one chilling comment from a young man at the end: 'I don't really want to know nothing more than I already know' but, apart from this, the comments from teachers and children have been very encouraging. The children were still full of eager questions and ideas at the end of the term's work, a sure sign of their awakened interest and enthusiasm.

Some of the schools involved have now included prehistory in their local history study unit, or as part of the 'enhanced curriculum'. The children visiting both Stonehenge and Avebury came to understand that the Stones with which they were comparatively familiar can only be understood in the context of their landscapes. World Heritage means something to them now and so does the value of their own heritage.

Evaluation of learning is notoriously difficult and time alone will tell whether these children grow up to be adults with an interest in the past, and a will to conserve their heritage. But the prospects look good. The Stonehenge and Avebury World Heritage Site Education Project seems to have been time and partnership well spent.

Bibliography

Anderson, C, Planel, P, and Stone, P, 2003 *Stonehenge, A Teacher's Guide*, Revised edition, English Heritage

Corbishley, M, Darvill, T, and Stone, P, 2000 *Prehistory, a Teacher's Guide*, English Heritage

Department for Education and Employment, 2000 *The National Curriculum Handbook for Primary Teachers Key Stages 1 & 2*, Qualifications and Curriculum Authority

Durbin, G, Morris, S, and Wilkinson, S, 1996 *Learning From Objects, A Teacher's Guide*, Revised edition, English Heritage

English Heritage, 2001 *The Historic Environment: A Force for our Future*

Henson, D, Stone, P, Corbishley, M, 2004 *Education and the Historic Environment*, Routledge

Wheatley, G, 1997 *World Heritage Sites, A Teacher's Guide*, English Heritage

Websites

WHS website: http://whc.unesco.org/
UNESCO World Heritage in Young Hands:
    http://whc.unesco.org/education/
QCA website: http://www.qca.org.uk/7.html
Wessex Arch website:
    http://www.wessexarch.co. uk
ASPnet: http://www.cewc.org/aspnet/profile.html
English Heritage:
    http://www.english-heritage.org. uk
National Trust: http://www.nationaltrust.org.uk

Research Frameworks for UK World Heritage Sites

Dave Batchelor

Before turning to the specific aspect of World Heritage Sites in the UK it is sensible to have a brief look at research frameworks in the wider context.

The wish or need to create frameworks to set and guide priorities for archaeological investigation has been recognised for 70 – 80 years. This can be traced back to the late 1920's when the Congress of Archaeological Societies discussed the amount of fieldwork currently underway and suggested that this should be co-ordinated to try to ensure a more equitable distribution of efforts (Peers 1929). The publication by English Heritage in 1996 of *Frameworks for our Past*, (Olivier 1996), is the latest in this sequence.

The team working on *Frameworks for our Past* undertook a survey of research frameworks and managed to locate some 727 documents that fell into the parameters of the project. These ranged in scope and content from short journal articles to altogether more ambitious pieces of work covering national, regional, and local aspects together with thematic and period based studies. It is worth noting that the documents fall into two almost exactly equal parts with 51% falling into the national category and 49% falling into the regional or local categories. It should also be noted that the survey focused on England although there were a very small number which ranged beyond and there were a few documents submitted that focused on the other home countries.

Having looked at the database created I cannot find any of the documents which relate specifically to any of the World Heritage Sites (WHS). In one sense this is not unexpected, as the UK did not nominate any sites until 1986. However, there are several, which encompass one or more WHS. Some of these are national in coverage, such as the Prehistoric Society's 1984 *Prehistory, Priorities and Society: the way for forward* and the Society for the Promotion of Roman Studies' 1985 *Priorities for the Preservation and excavation of Romano-British Sites*. Others are thematic, such as Roebuck and Davison's 1995 *Medieval Monastic Sites: priorities for research*, or regional like Clack and Gosling's 1976 *Archaeology in the North, Northern Archaeological Survey*.

Olivier attempted to bring about some order in the use of terms and suggests a set of definitions. This has led to the now familiar division into Resource Assessment (past), Research Agenda (present) and Research Strategy (future). The resource assessment is a factual account of the current state of knowledge and understanding which is draws heavily upon the extant Sites and Monuments Records/ Historic Environment Records. The research agenda identifies gaps in the knowledge, assesses the potential of the resource and takes account of externally derived research topics. The research strategy then takes the previous stages and develops this into a prioritised list of objectives. These three elements are then combined to form a Research Framework.

At English Heritage, the outcome of Olivier's work has been a number of funded programmes to address some of the conclusions he reached. English Heritage has encouraged the development of regional research frameworks for the nine government regions as a matter priority. These are seen as important in supporting the implementation of PPG 16, and to a lesser extent of PPG 15.[1] The nine regional frameworks are at different stages of development, with the East of England leading the way, and all vary slightly in their scope and content. In addition, English Heritage has funded a number of national frameworks addressing thematic or period topics, such as wetlands archaeology or Roman archaeology.

Whilst English Heritage has been concentrating its resources on regional and national aspects, it has also been funding projects to develop Research Frameworks for more discrete and smaller geographic areas. It is fair to say that this is usually in response to, and associated with, a management need. The Research Framework for the Greater Thames Estuary (Williams and Brown 1999) is an example of this, as are the Research Frameworks for Avebury and Stonehenge.

Turning now to the World Heritage Site context, it is first important to note where research fits within UNESCO and World Heritage Centre documentation. The term 'research' first occurs in Article 5 of the *Convention Concerning the Protection of the World Cultural and Natural Heritage* (UNESCO 1972). Article 5 states that:

> To ensure that effective and active measures are taken for the protection, conservation and presentation of the cultural and natural heritage situated on its territory, each State Party to this Convention shall endeavour, in so far as possible, and as appropriate for each country:

> [Subsection (c)] ... to develop scientific and technical studies and research and to work out such operating methods as will make the State capable of

---

[1] Planning Policy Guidance (PPG) Notes 15 (1994) and 16 (1990) published by the Department of the Environment, set out the broad policy framework within which archaeology and the built heritage respectively are protected within the planning process.

counteracting the dangers that threaten its cultural or natural heritage;.

and

[Subsection (e)] *... to foster the establishment or development of national or regional centres for training in the protection, conservation and presentation of the cultural and natural heritage and to encourage scientific research in this field.*

This reference is then reinforced in paragraph 215 of the *Operational Guidelines for the Implementation of the World Heritage Convention* (UNESCO 2005), which states:

The Committee develops and co-ordinates international co-operation in the area of research needed for the effective implementation of the Convention. States Parties are also encouraged to make resources available to undertake research, since knowledge and understanding are fundamental to the identification, management, and monitoring of World Heritage properties.

The guidelines for the management of World Heritage Sites published for UNESCO (Feilden and Jokilehto, 1993) recommended the establishment of a research co-ordination committee for individual World Heritage Sites within the overall management structures for the site. It is suggested that the role of this committee is to devise research programmes and promote and co-ordinate research in the area.

It is in this context that research objectives are then picked up in the individual World Heritage Site management plans. A quick scan of those management plans on the ICOMOS UK web site show that many make specific reference to research in the their objectives.

I now want to take a quick look at three WHS research frameworks, all which were published within the last five years. It may well have something to do with the prominence given to the archaeology, and therefore to archaeologists, in the management of these particular sites that they have been the first ones to embrace the concept of a research framework for the WHS. I am aware that work is currently underway on developing a Research Framework for Hadrian's Wall but not for many of the other sites in the UK at least.

This self-selected group of Avebury, Orkney and Stonehenge make for an interesting case study of how research frameworks can be developed and implemented. These sites share a number of common factors in addition to the WHS inscription. Not least amongst these is a shared Neolithic and Bronze Age date and the fact they comprise a number of monuments spread over a considerable geographic area.

Taking these in order of publication and starting with Avebury, it is fair to say that this represents a transitional document with much thinking and some writing being undertaken prior to the publication of *Frameworks for our Past*. This is by no means a criticism but merely a reflection of the circumstances. The Avebury Archaeological and Historic Research

Group (AAHRG), who were instrumental in bringing this to publication, came into being formally in 1993, although many individuals making up its membership had been meeting together since about 1990. The appearance of *Frameworks for our Past* in 1996 led to renewed effort and gave a structure to be followed (Olivier 1996). At about the same time there was a complimentary stimulus which led to the development of the first Avebury WHS management plan (English Heritage 1998). This picked up on the first draft of the research framework, recognising the high potential for further research and probably more importantly, the fundamental link between research and the overall management of Avebury.

The Avebury research agenda uses a chronological framework with eight divisions, starting with the Lower and Middle Palaeolithic and running through to the Medieval period. Each division is repeated in the resource assessment, research agenda and research strategies sections with the same author or authors responsible for all three sections. In addition, there are a number of thematic elements, such as palaeo-environmental evidence, which supplement the chronological divisions. Concluding the volume, there is a separate chapter which explores the potential use of a number of different methods and techniques such as aerial photography and geophysical survey.

In producing a research framework for a WHS, AARHG and the individual authors had to break new ground. As far as I am aware the Avebury research framework (Chadburn and Pomeroy-Kellinger 2001) when it was published was the first and only such document for any WHS world-wide.

The Research Agenda for the Heart of Neolithic Orkney (Downs *et al.* 2005) was published by Historic Scotland and represents the culmination of a process which began in 2001. The project began with the establishment of an Archaeological and Historical Research Co-ordination Committee (AHRCC) which then organised a symposium in Orkney. The principle aim behind this symposium was to set out and agree the research issues. A number of working parties were set up which addressed issues such as landscape, monuments and cultural identity.

This research framework has encompassed the maritime environment and in comparison with the Avebury document has included more artefact-based aspects and drawn in the museum collections. It has also embraced the more ephemeral aspects of the WHS such as folklore and perceptions of the landscape. In doing so, and in comparison to Avebury, it has broadened the scope to include recent and modern periods.

The research framework for Stonehenge (English Heritage 2005) was started in April 2001 when Tim Darvill of Bournemouth University was appointed to oversee its co-ordination. It is fair to say that whilst the need for such a document for Stonehenge had been accepted for many years, it had not risen high enough up the list of priorities because of other issues such as the management plan, roads improvement and visitor centre plan, which had diverted time and effort.

The development of the Stonehenge document started with a series of open meetings, which served much the same purpose as the Orkney Symposium in determining the range and content of the framework. These meetings were followed up with the wide circulation of draft documents and by the establishment of a dedicated web site which generated additional comment.

The stated aims of the Stonehenge framework were slightly wider than those for Avebury and Orkney. As well aiming to raise awareness of the importance of research and encourage focused research, as the others had, it also aimed to maximise research opportunities from all potential ground disturbance, stimulate new and dynamic approaches, and inform presentation of the site to the public. Other differences or modifications from the Avebury document included a wider coverage of all periods from the Palaeolithic to the 20th century and a stress on the need for problem-orientated research.

Although the Stonehenge framework used a similar four-part format as in the earlier examples, it was rather more sophisticated and detailed in the presentation of the data. For example, Part 3 (research agenda) is presented as series of 37 issues based on four themes:

- period & site based issues e.g. how was Stonehenge built?
- Subject based issues e.g. landscape evolution & design
- Contextual & interpretative issues e.g. the meaning of monument classifications
- Management based issues e.g. linking research & site management

Similarly, the twenty-five research objectives presented in Part 4 (linked back to the issues) in 5 themed groups:

- The big questions (e.g. how, why and when)
- Stonehenge & related monuments
- Landscape & regional objectives
- Integrating monuments & the landscape
- Research infrastructure (implementation)

In developing the framework for Stonehenge it was necessary to extend it beyond the scope of normal archaeological interests. This has included themes such as the archaeoastronomical aspects which have a considerable body of literature and current following. The development of these research frameworks has brought to light a number of other issues which should be addressed in future with respect to World Heritage Sites. These include:

- Within the World Heritage Centre Operational Guidelines the references to research should be broadened from the current management/scientific context to include the academic context.
- What is needed is the establishment of an archaeological/historical research committee within the overall management structure for each WHS. I would suggest that it is then up to the committee to ensure that the research aspects are adequately covered, either within a specific research framework or within a broader framework that encompasses the values of the WHS.
- The research framework should be as inclusive as possible and include all aspects relevant to those with an interest in the WHS. This is not just to capture those less mainstream elements but to include those aspects which usually sit underneath the management banner.

Finally, one of the indicators of the success for a research framework should be the interest created and new information generated by it. This should then lead onto a revision of the framework and a refocusing of the strategy. A number of research frameworks are currently under review and revision, including those for the Greater Thames Estuary and Avebury.

Bibliography

Chadburn, A, and Pomeroy-Kellinger, M, (eds) 2001 *Archaeological Research Agenda for the Avebury World Heritage Site*, Avebury Archaeological Research Group, Trust for Wessex Archaeology/ English Heritage

Clack, P, and Gosling, P, 1976 *Archaeology in the North*, Northern Archaeological Survey, Durham

Downs, J, Foster, S, and Wickham-Jones, C (eds) 2005 *The Heart of Neolithic Orkney World Heritage Site Research Agenda*, Historic Scotland

English Heritage, 1998 *Avebury World Heritage Site Management Plan*

English Heritage, 2005 *Stonehenge World Heritage Site: An Archaeological Research Framework*

Feilden, B, and Jokilehto, J, 1993 *Management guidelines for world heritage sites*, 1st edition, UNESCO/ ICOMOS/ICCROM, Rome

Olivier, A, 1996 *Frameworks for Our Past: A Review of Research Frameworks, Strategies and Perceptions*, English Heritage.

Peers, C, 1929 A Regional Policy for fieldwork, *Antiquaries Journal* **9**, 349–353

Prehistoric Society, 1984 *Prehistory, Priorities and Society: the way for forward*

Roebuck, J, and Davison, A, 1995 *Medieval Monastic Sites: priorities for research*, Unpublished internal document, English Heritage

Society for the Promotion of Roman Studies, 1985 *Priorities for the Preservation and Excavation of Romano-British sites*, London

UNESCO 1972 *Convention Concerning the Protection of the World Cultural and Natural Heritage.* Website: http://whc.unesco.org/en/conventiontext/

UNESCO 2005 *Operational Guidelines for the Implementation of the World Heritage Convention*, Paris: UNESCO, World Heritage Centre, WHC.05/2 (2 February 2005)

Williams, J, and Brown, N, 1999 *An archaeological research framework for the Greater Thames Estuary*, English Heritage, Essex County Council and Kent County Council.

Niuheliang, Liaoning Province, People's Republic of China: Strategies for the Management of a Complex Cultural Landscape

Tim Williams

INTRODUCTION

Niuheliang is an extensive cultural landscape, primarily comprising a series of Neolithic sites located on the border of Lingyuan County and Jianping County in Liaoning Province in northeast China (41° 20′ N and 119° 30′ E). The landscape covers an area of more than 50 km^2, perhaps extending to an area as large as 80 km^2. The sites date from the Hongshan Culture (*c* 4,500–2,900 BCE), which was first identified in the 1920s. The cultural landscape currently encompasses sixteen known monument groups (referred to by the excavators as Locations 1–16; see LPIACR 2004, fig 3; Barnes & Guo 1996, fig 2), which include substantial burial mounds, satellite burials, large hillside platforms, 'altars' and 'temples', within a river valley system ringed by mountains. No settlement sites have yet been discovered, although evidence suggests largely sedentary communities, agriculturalists who cultivated millet and pigs for subsistence, and accomplished artisans who carved jade and made thin black-on-red pottery. The Niuheliang landscape lies roughly at the centre of the known distribution of Hongshan sites.

The landscape has been actively excavated and researched since 1981 (Guo 1995; LPIACR 1997 & 2004) primarily under the direction of Professor Guo Dashun, who was at the time the Director of the Provincial Institute of Archaeology, and now by the Liaoning Provincial Cultural Relics Archaeological Research Institute, led by Prof Zhu Da. The site was declared one of the 'Top Ten Archaeological Discoveries of 2003 in China'. The landscape is one of fifty-five sites currently on the People's Republic of China World Heritage Site tentative list.

THE MONUMENT COMPLEX

The monuments identified thus far include:

- **Burial mounds:** usually earthen mounds with stone revetting, facing; ranging from 300m^2 to over 1,000m^2; often with a central stone cist grave (primary burial), surrounded by secondary/satellite burials; various layouts including round, square, combined circle-square structures; outer boundaries to some mounds constructed of painted cylindrical ceramic vessels; graves with single or multiple occupants; rich grave goods.
- **Artificial hill** (Location 13): a substantial artificial mound of earth with stone revetting and kerb.
- **'Altars'**: round earthen structures revetted with stone, with central stone platforms, interpreted as altars.
- **'Goddess Temple'** (Location 1): two buildings; largest c 18m long, slightly irregular rectangular plan with side 'chambers', max width 7m; smaller building 6 x 2m; semi-subterranean structure; wattle, daub & timber walls; evidence of painted interior walls, with triangular geometric patterns in reddish brown, interlaced with yellow and white; associated clay statuary, including so-called 'Goddess' figure with jade eyes, jade objects and pottery.
- **Platforms**: substantial hillside stone built platforms; surrounding the 'Goddess Temple'.

Associated material includes jade and turquoise objects, painted cylindrical ceramic vessels, other ceramic vessels, large quantities of pig bone, several fragmentary unbaked clay statues and possible evidence for copper smelting. The clay statues were all excavated from the 'Goddess Temple' and range from half life size to three times life size. They include part of a female human with inlaid jade eyes (the so-called 'Goddess') and animal forms. The copper smelting evidence (copper-smelting crucibles with attached slag were found, as was a copper earring in a tomb (Tiemei *et al.* 1998) may push copper smelting in north-east China back to as early as 2500 BCE (Kresten *et al.* 2003, 12).

INTER-VISIBILITY OF MONUMENTS AND THE 'CEREMONIAL' LANDSCAPE

Clearly an important design element was the visibility and inter-visibility of the monument complexes within the landscape. Most of the burial mounds are sited on low hills within the valley system, with clear lines of sight between specific monuments: for example, the most substantial mound (Location 13) lies at a cross axis of views to mounds (Locations 12, 14/15 and 16), and the 'Goddess Temple' (Location 1).

It has also been suggested that a distinctive natural feature, a low mountain with a profile shaped like a sleeping animal, either a 'Boar' or 'Bear' (Fig. 1), was also incorporated into the visual setting and organisation of the landscape, forming as it does a visual marker at the opposing end of the complex from the 'Goddess Temple' (Location 1) (Barnes and Guo 1996; Guo 1997; LPIACR 2004). Guo has suggested

Figure 1 'Boar' or 'Bear' mountain, viewed from the mounds at Location 5.

that the line of sight between the two forms the axis of the landscape, with other monuments set out in relation to this (*loc cit*).

Archaeo-astronomical attributes of the landscape have also been explored:

> calculations and analysis of the localities at Niuheliang, declination angles corresponding to both significant solar and lunar angles as well as possessing some distinguishing factor about their location or contents were analyzed to highlight promising alignments between the heavens and the terrestrial landscape (Nelson *et al.* n.d., 7).

No residential sites have been found within, or close to, the Niuheliang complex (Guo 1997), suggesting that it was a sacred place separated from everyday secular life. The discovery of this landscape, with its complex burial monuments, combined with possible ceremonial aspects, provides the first indications of developed mortuary ritual, perhaps suggesting some sort of governing ideology or way of thinking about the afterlife. At present this makes the Hongshan Culture different from other Neolithic groups identified in China. There is also considerable debate as to whether this landscape also provides indications of the development of different social classes.

THE CURRENT LANDSCAPE AND THE CONDITION OF THE ARCHAEOLOGICAL REMAINS

The landscape currently encompasses agricultural land (largely confined to the lower part of the valley bottom, and some of the lower slopes) and managed pine forests (mainly on the middle and upper slopes, including the designated Niuheliang Forest Park) (Fig. 2). There is little or no habitation within the valley, although there are substantial centres of population nearby, such as Lingyuan which lies 9 km north-east with a population of *c* 150,000. A minor road runs along the valley bottom while a new highway linking Beijing (280 kms to the southwest) to Shenyang in the north-east, is currently under construction and due to open in 2007 in advance of the 2008 Olympic Games. The route will run through one of the adjacent valley systems, but a service station junction will provide access to the Niuheliang landscape. A railway line also runs through the valley bottom, in places in a steep cutting.

Figure 2   The valley landscape of managed pine forest, terraced agriculture and low hill ridges, each of which is surmounted by a Neolithic monument.

The spectacular excavated sites present a challenge for site management. Most of the excavated sites are deteriorating rapidly, which is not surprising given the harsh climatic conditions in the region and the relatively fragile nature of the archaeological resource, especially the earthen structures. They are suffering considerable deterioration due to rain washing away earthen material and freeze/thaw cycles damaging the stones.

Some of the sites have been partially backfilled, giving some protection to the most vulnerable material, and a shelter was erected at the 'Goddess Temple' (Location 1) to protect the site from rainfall and provide some security.

In the summer temperatures can reach a maximum 36° to 40°C, whereas in winter they can drop as low as −29.5°C, with average minimum temperatures of −15° to −18°C. Heavy rainfall takes place in the late autumn/early winter, with snow throughout the winter months. The exposed stone is particularly susceptible to frost damage, occurring when the stone becomes frozen whilst very wet, leading to cracking and shattering of the stone (Price 2006) (Fig. 3).

Rainfall is also causing erosion to the earthen mounds. When unexcavated, these are stabilised by plant growth, especially grasses. But after excavation the earthen mounds are subject to small scale slippage and destabilisation, a problem which is accentuated by the ancient construction process of using stone fragments to revet or cover the earthen mounds. This technique was probably effective when maintained in antiquity, and perhaps consolidated with vegetation, but in its exposed 'just excavated' condition, the soil washes out, destabilising the structure and leading to stone tumble and slippage.

Small-scale plant growth is evident at many sites. In the main this is problematic for obscuring features and decreasing the aesthetic and interpretative value of the monuments, but in places the vegetation roots are causing damage to the buried deposits especially on partially excavated sites or those with a thin covering of loose backfill.

Tree growth is more problematic: not only are the root systems potentially more damaging, but later tree fall/felling can cause significant damage through the root ball lift. This is particularly

Figure 3 The outer kerb of Mound 4 at Location 2. This type of stone, perhaps micaceous, is particularly susceptible to freeze/thaw cycles, and has deteriorated very rapidly since exposure.

problematic on incompletely back-filled excavations, where trees are attracted by the greater moisture in the unconsolidated excavation trenches. Animal activity is also noticeable, again attracted to the unconsolidated fills of old excavations.

Agricultural activities have been excluded from known monument complexes. Crucially, however, there is an incomplete understanding of the location and extent of the buried archaeological resource, and it is likely that valuable elements of the Neolithic landscape lie within the area of current agricultural land.

Forestry is an important part of the local economy and large areas of the valley are covered with managed pine forests. The extent of the Platforms around the 'Goddess Temple' (Location 1) is still incompletely understood, a situation compounded the under-management of large areas that are planted with forestry. Managing the forestry will require careful collaboration, not just with the forestry industry but also with the recreational and environmental interests in the landscape.

Numerous deep drainage channels cut through the hillside of the valley, carrying seasonal heavy rains down the slopes. These require mapping, probably using high resolution satellite imagery,

and their potential impact on the archaeological sites should be assessed and monitored.

CURRENT SITE MANAGEMENT

Since the early 2000s there have been some efforts to develop a management response to the landscape, where previously archaeological investigation had taken priority.

A shelter, with surrounding drainage scheme and security fence, was constructed at the 'Goddess Temple' (Location 1) immediately after excavation, and has clearly been effective in protecting the site. It requires some minor repairs, and there are issues to consider in terms of interpretation and landscape setting (below), but in general it has enabled the site to be preserved and displayed. Some excavations were partially reburied. It is likely that these have been effective, at least partially, in helping to alleviate the worse of the rain and freeze/thaw problems. However, the unconsolidated nature of the back-filling tends to attract moisture, plants, and animal activity, and has not stopped other erosion problems (notably the collapse of sections and trench edges).

The Institute of Chinese Cultural Heritage undertook some experimental conservation at Niuheliang to characterise the stone and earth, and evaluate treatments for remedial conservation. It did not deal in depth with the mechanisms of decay nor with possible preventive approaches. Generally, there has been little success at finding products for the impregnation/consolidation of earthen structures, and procedures for evaluating their effectiveness are notoriously unreliable. Similarly, no products have been found that will reliably prevent frost damage in exposed stone. Such products have usually been intended to prevent the penetration of water, and thereby remove all possibility of ice formation inside the stone. In practice, however, they may also have the effect of trapping in any water that may penetrate into the stone, so that the water content is increased, not reduced. A more reliable approach to the prevention of frost damage is to keep the stone above freezing point by providing shelter that will protect if from rain. This approach is discussed below.

The World Bank supported some work on mounds at Location 2, including the construction of stone paths for visitors (Fig. 4) and a substantial stone platform. Unfortunately both of these are visually damaging to the setting of the site.

A Management Plan has been prepared for the Niuheliang landscape by the National Bureau of Cultural Relics, which has been adopted at National and Provincial level, although there are currently no plans or resources to implement the scheme. The lan suggested that the mounds at Location 2 be displayed without a shelter, but as discussed below, this would severely limit the scale, quality and effectiveness of the site presentation and conservation.

Figure 4 One of the paths built under the World Bank programme. The path is hard wearing and clear, and built in a very different material to the monuments.

Unfortunately, however, path runs very close to the edge of the mound, severely detracting from its setting and visually dominating the monument. To further damage the interpretative impact, the line of the kerb of the monument has been 'marked out' using the same stones as the path (to the right of the photograph): while this might superficially aid interpretation, in fact it is likely to confuse, with the path stones now integrated into the monument, and the distinction between intervention and archaeological fabric blurred.

A SUGGESTED WAY FORWARD – MANAGING NEOLITHIC MONUMENTS IN THE CURRENT LANDSCAPE (FIG. 5)

Key principles

There are three key principles that might underpin a way forward for the management of this internationally important landscape.

1 **Cultural landscape:** the concept and definition of the area as a cultural landscape (with important issues of time, depth, definition, boundaries), rather than seeing it as a number of isolated funerary or ritual monuments. Such an approach would integrate landscape management and local needs with increased visitor impacts, and focus interpretation as a landscape experience, albeit situated and viewed from specific locations.
2 **An holistic approach to management:** the need for integrated planning that encompasses conservation, interpretation, education, visitor manage-

ment, active research, ecology, and the needs of the local community.
3 **Participatory planning:** relevant organisations and communities must be integrated into the planning process if the strategies to be devised and implemented are to be sustainable.

It is essential that **small scale preventative conservation measures** are put in place as soon as possible. These need not be expensive nor complex to implement, but would help to ensure that this internationally important resource survives while plans and decisions over its long-term conservation and display are resolved, and appropriate resources raised for effective implementation. As far as is possible, these short-term actions should be reversible.

Other key issues include the boundary of the landscape, buffer zones (especially associated with the visual and landscape setting of the site), and the potential impact, upon the landscape, visitor facilities, and the local community, of any future World Heritage status.

Conservation: monitoring, research & diagnosis

There is no magic solution for the conservation and protection of these sites if they open to the harsh elements of the area. The devastating and rapid loss that these spectacular sites are suffering cannot be halted with a simple spray-on solution. Chemical consolidants have been explored and have had some minor success, but the two key factors involved in the deterioration of these sites – rain washing away earthen material and freeze/thaw cycles damaging the stones – cannot be resolved if they remain exposed.

Where it is not essential for the archaeological remains to be exposed for interpretative purposes, for example at the artificial hill (Location 13), re-burial would seem to be the most cost-effective, efficient, sustainable and reversible option. It may even enhance some interpretative options, such as monument visibility within the landscape (below).

Where the remains are of such visual or associative significance that their display is considered to be essential, perhaps most obviously in the case at the 'Goddess Temple', the Platforms, and the outstanding complex of monuments at Location 2, then shelters are probably the only practical way forward. Protecting the soil from erosion will remain fundamentally about protecting it from rain. Stopping the freeze/thaw cycle, which is so damaging to the stones, is not about stopping the stone from freezing – that is impractical given the low winter temperatures and would require substantial energy – but rather about stopping the stones from becoming saturated in the first place.

Shelters

The negative aspects of shelter construction at archaeological sites are well known, and such works

Figure 5   The complex current landscape of archaeological features, in various stages of decay and excavation, modern agriculture, and tree planting, all set against dramatic topographic change.

cannot be taken lightly at Locations 1 & 2. Most obviously any shelters at the site would have a tremendous visual impact upon the landscape and as such would necessarily intrude into the otherwise rural, unbuilt character of the area. However, there are also strengths and opportunities to the use of shelters in this context:

- Visitor focus (see interpretation below) – focusing on the locations that most visitors will want to see (Locations 1 & 2). Shelters do tend to draw people to specific points in the landscape; here that could and should be part of the interpretation strategy.
- It is difficult at Location 2 to understand the layout and scale of the mounds. An aerial or elevated viewpoint is more effective in understanding the scale of the complex, although obviously this was not the original viewpoint for seeing the structures. But then neither is the eroded state in which they are now found their original state. A shelter could provide elevated viewpoints to enable a better understanding of the layout and connection of the mounds within this complex. (Fig. 6)
- Shelters offer the opportunity to present interpretative material and their interpretative performance

should be seen as a key design issue. Simple shelters can provide space for durable panels, while more elaborate shelters can also provide secure display space for associated material culture. The quality of the material culture at Niuheliang is outstanding, and it would clearly be desirable to be able to present some of it in close association with its context. The balance between on-site display and display within an interpretation centre for the whole landscape would need to be carefully considered, taking into account security and staffing issues (see below).

Other design issues might include:

- Ensuring that the structures enabled visitors to look out from the Location 2 area; using design features to focus interactions on enabling, rather than blocking, landscape connectivity.
- Deciding whether the objective is to blend into the landscape, using features such as grass roofs, or whether the objective is not to blend into the landscape but to denote the location of this clearly key complex of monuments, making it visible to other locations within the ceremonial landscape in

Figure 6   The current low level view makes the layout and scale of the monuments difficult for the visitor to understand.

an echo of the way it might have been in its original form.

- The conservation priority of the shelter should be to provide a dry, well ventilated, environment; solar panels could also be used to provide energy for essential services.
- Reversibility – ensuring that it is possible to remove the shelters without physical damage to the site (although clearly the strategy would not be financially reversible).

A possible variant on the strategy would be to use temporary seasonal shelters that could be removed during the spring, summer and early autumn. There have been considerable advances in high tensile steel and textile structures. Temporary structures would also be smaller, and perhaps could be used to mimic the scale of the monuments in the landscape.

With either permanent or temporary shelters, it is important that full consideration is given to their maintenance; they do not represent a cost-neutral process, even once funds for construction have been raised. In addition, all shelters have a security issue, especially more elaborate structures with facilities such as on-site material culture displays and solar panels.

Reburial as part of conservation and interpretative strategies

Earthen architecture exposed in the course of archaeological excavation presents particular problems for both archaeologist and conservator. The abandonment of non back-filled trenches after excavation, can lead to disastrous consequences. Reburial requires a carefully planned and implemented strategy, which is cognisant of issues of documentation, trench and interface preparation, and preparation of fill material, compaction, drainage, visual impacts and monitoring (see Cooke in press).

While Locations 1 & 2 are considered suitable for display, permanent, well designed and implemented reburial needs to take place at Locations, 3, 4, 5 and 13. Most sites being reburied would be restored to their pre-excavation (degraded) state. The visual setting of the monument in the Neolithic appears to have been an integral part of their design. The interpretation of the monuments in a landscape context might be aided, if some of the mounds were 'reconstructed' as part of their reburial strategy, making their visual presence easier to interpret for visitors and making it easier to assess their impact from distance. For example the reconstructed

Figure 7 Location 2 seen from Location 3. Location 2 was a dramatic complex of monuments laid out along a slight terrace at the base of the hillside.

mounds at Sutton Hoo, England (Carver 1998, 160-1) or the major Neolithic monument at Newgrange, Ireland (Stout 2002, 43-5), provide a useful interpretative tool giving the opportunity to consider the original scale and impact of the monuments, and also for the visitor to understand the degraded state of the unreconstructed mounds.

The mounds at Location 3 are in need of protective reburial. They are easily visible from Location 2, which would be one of the main visitor centres, but physically separated by the railway line. Location 3 has little that can be effectively displayed in-situ. Creating a visible feature within the landscape here would enable visitors to Location 2 to consider the landscape interaction of the sites, without the need to cross the railway line. The site could provide a dramatic opportunity to interpret the scale and form of the mounds to the visitor. Again, restoration would be easily reversible. A longer walking route to Location 3, taking in Locations 4 & 5, could form part of a landscape walk for those visitors prepared to spend longer exploring the area.

There are obviously a number of problems with reconstruction, not least the quality of evidence available to interpret original height, covering, whether the kerbs were exposed, etc. Partial rebuilding can itself be misleading, because it gives the visitor a confusing message that is neither the original height of the mound in Neolithic, as now interpreted, nor the eroded form that was present in the contemporary landscape before excavation.

A key feature of any interpretation or presentation strategy will be the need to take account of the intervisibility of the monument complexes (Fig. 7).

New research

Understanding the extent of the monument complexes, and the survival of below-ground archaeological resources, is clearly important to developing approaches towards the management of this landscape. In 2002 Prof Guo Dashun (Liaoning Province Archaeological Research Institute) and Dr Sarah Nelson (University of Denver, Colorado) undertook a remote sensing project at Niuheliang. They conducted ground penetrating radar (GPR) and geophysical surveys in the 'Platforms' area, producing maps, 3-D models of buried features, and GPS reference points (Bell *et al.* 2002). The results of this work will be important in establishing a strategy for the management of the landscape with the Platforms and the 'Goddess Temple' (Location 1), although additional survey work may be needed to establish the survival of buried resources and the effective boundaries to site and land management schemes.

The information platform for decision-making needs to be enhanced by various means including digital terrain modelling, to enable inter-visibility studies both for interpretation and management planning/design (including shelter construction); acquisition & analysis of high resolution satellite imagery and aerial photography; GIS development and the collation of existing archival information.

Further excavation of the 'Goddess Temple' (Location 1) would be very important in exploring the nature of the structures and the associated practices at the site. However, the potential complexity of the excavation, the quantity of material, and its fragile nature, need careful consideration before the logistics of such an operation can be considered. Issues such as sampling strategies, retrieval and analysis methodologies (for example, lifting and refitting issues, photogrammetric recording, 3D modelling, laser scanning, computer modelling), conservation, storage, curation and display all need consideration.

Landscape and vegetation management

The Platforms area requires careful tree felling, once the extent of the buried resources is understood. This will need to be done in close liaison with the forestry authorities, and new plant growth effectively monitored and managed in the future. Elsewhere, very selective tree felling might be considered to both manage the close environs of monument complexes and, especially, to enable lines of sight between monuments to be maintained or reopened. Work on a digital terrain model would also assist in planning this process.

The management of agricultural activities needs to be carefully reviewed in collaboration with the local community and based upon additional research into the extent of buried archaeological resources and site boundaries. The recreational and environmental aspects of landscape management also need to be fully integrated into the overall management strategies for the landscape, including the nature of the interpretational process.

Interpretation and education strategy

Currently we have little idea of likely visitor dwell time. Most non-local visitors will probably not spend a great deal of time in the landscape. Options should be developed that enable relatively short visits (which would probably focus on Locations 1 and 2 where the best preserved material would be on view), with the rest of the monuments viewed from a distance. For some visitors, especially local people and education groups, longer visits should be planned for, extending out into the landscape (walks, paths, integrating ecological and environmental issues, activity-based learning strategies, etc). This could involve leading people to different aspects of the landscape – for example the view from Location 3 which enables the viewer to appreciate the sheltered position of the Location 2 complex on a low lying plateau (Fig. 7).

Local education must be a priority: local schools represent a large potential audience and by diversifying the experience, away from simply the main monuments or indeed just archaeological interpretation, the landscape could provide an enormously rich educational experience. This could do much to promote the sustainability of the site with the local community.

The construction and location of interpretation centres – whether single or multi-focal – will require considerable planning and consultation. Again, new build options bring in considerations of the visual impact upon the landscape. Using existing structures (such as the school adjacent to the study centre) may be both cost-effective and reduce impact. They might also provide good education facilities. As discussed above, using new shelter design to incorporate aspects of a visitor centre might also have benefits.

Highway 101 between Beijing and Shenyang, currently under construction, could radically alter the potential of the landscape to attract foreign and national tourists. A service station designated to provide access to the landscape, and perhaps some interpretation, could attract more short-stay visitors.

Management planning

In developing effective strategies, and a workable and sustainable management plan, it will be essential to form effective partnerships, with a participatory framework that draws in the local community and local education interests. An effective management structure will also need to be in place. This should be concerned not only with the development and implementation of strategies but also with the long-term status and operation of activities at the site.

The long-term economic sustainability of the approaches developed will need to be assessed. It is often easier to raise funds for capital expenditure than for long-term staffing and maintenance: the future funding for interpretation centres, education programmes, shelters, monitoring, etc, needs to be considered. Potentially the new Highway 101 and the possibility of some foreign tourism might create a sustainable model, but only if some of the resources generated by that process remain with the landscape/park. And, importantly, the impact of drawing these new visitors to the area, both Chinese and foreign, especially when the new road provides better transportation links, needs to be carefully explored with the local authorities and community.

CONCLUSIONS

The solution to managing this complex landscape probably involves a reburial programme for most of the excavated sites, explicitly linked to a landscape interpretation strategy. The exceptions would be the development of the display and interpretation of the 'Goddess Temple' (Location 1) and the surrounding Platforms, and the complex of monuments at Location 2. The only sustainable strategy for displaying these sites would seem to involve sheltering. These sites would provide the focus for most short- or medium-duration visitors, while longer visits, especially from the local community and for educational purposes, could be planned to take advantage of the wider landscape. The shelters could perform a number of interpretive functions beyond simply providing preventative conservation.

It is essential that small scale preventative conservation measures are put in place as soon as possible. These need not be expensive, nor complex to implement, but would help to ensure that this internationally important resource survives whilst plans and decisions over its long-term conservation and display are resolved, and appropriate resources raised for effective implementation. All short-term actions should be reversible.

Bibliography

Abbreviations: LPIACR = Liaoning Provincial Institute of Archaeology and Cultural Relics
IPPA = Indo-Pacific Prehistory Association

Barnes, G & Guo, D, 1996 The ritual landscape of the "Boar Mountain" Basin: the Niuheliang site complex of north-eastern China, *World Archaeol* **28** (2), 209–19

Bell, C, Guo, D, Lu, X, Martin-Montgomery, A, Nelson, S, Niu, H, Pak, Y, Tchakirides, T & Zhu, D, 2002 Geophysical Investigations at Niuheliang, China, Unpublished conference paper presented at *The 17th Congress of the Indo-Pacific Prehistory Association, Taipei.*

Carver, M, 1998 *Sutton Hoo. Burial ground of Kings?* London: British Museum Press

Cooke, L, in press *The archaeologist's challenge or despair: approaches to the reburial of archaeological sites at Merv, Turkmenistan,* Merv Technical Report 1. Institute of Archaeology, UCL. Heritage Marketing Publications

Guo, D, 1995 Hongshan and Related Cultures, in S M Nelson (ed) *The Archaeology of Northeast China,* London: Routledge, 21–64

Guo, D, 1997 Zhonghua wuqiannian wenming de xiangzheng (Symbol of the five-thousand years civilization of China), in Liaoningsheng wenwu kaogu yanjiusuo (eds) *Niuheliang Hongshan wenhua yizhi yu yuqi jingcui* (The Niuheliang site and Jade objects of the Hongshan culture). Beijing: Wenwu chubanshe, 1–48.

Kresten, P, Goedicke, C & Manzano, A, 2003 TL-dating of vitrified material, *Geochronometria* **22**, 9–14

LPIACR 1997 *Niu He Liang Ruins in Hongshan Culture,* Cultural Relics Publishing House

LPIACR 2004 *Niuheliang site,* Beijing: Academy Press

Li, X, 2002 Ritual and residential: the Bang and Laohushan river surveys, Inner Mongolia, *Bulletin of the Indo-Pacific Prehistory Association* **6**

Nelson, S M (ed) 1995a *The Archaeology of Northeast China: Beyond the Great Wall,* London: Routledge

Nelson, S M, 1995b Ritualised pigs and the origins of complex society: hypotheses regarding the Hongshan Culture, *Early China* **20**, 1–16

Nelson, S M, 1997 Hongshan: an early complex society in Northeast China, in Bellwood, P and Tillotson, D (eds), *Indo-Pacific Prehistory: The Chiang Mai Papers Volume 3,* Indo-Pacific Prehistory Association, 59–61

Nelson, S M, Matson, R A, Roberts R M, Rock, C & Stencel, R E, n.d. *Archaeoastronomical evidence for Wuism at the Hongshan site of Niuheliang,* available at https://www.portfolio.du.edu/pc/port2?page = 3&uid = 4768

Stout, G, 2002 *Newgrange and the bend of the Boyne.* Cork: Cork University Press

Price, C, 2006 Conservation problems, in Williams, T and Price, C, *Niuheliang, Liaoning Province. Technical report on site management options. Preliminary visit for the International Centre for Chinese Heritage and Archaeology.* Unpublished report Institute of Archaeology, UCL

Tiemei, C, Yanxiang, L and Wenbo, B, 1998 Dating of the copper-smelting remains found at Niuheliang site. *Proceedings the Fourth International Conference on the Beginning of the Use on Metals and Alloys (BUMA-IV),* 231–232

Underhill, A P, & Habu, J, 2006 Early communities in Asia, in M T Stark (ed) *Archaeology of Asia,* London: Blackwell, 121–148

Yan, W, 1999 Neolithic settlements in China: latest findings and research, *Journal of East Asian Archaeology* **1**, 131–147

World Heritage, Landscapes and Politics: Some Thoughts from Current Work

Peter Fowler

WORLD HERITAGE

In that 'wider perspective', World Heritage itself, something which was conceptualised in hope but which has always carried doubts, is now the subject of severe and fundamental criticism as we move from simple questions about how many World Heritage sites do we need to the public questioning of what it is for and what it is actually achieving. Interestingly, much of this critical interest arises from management issues. It is no coincidence that such critiques, internal as well as more obviously external, come in the wake of the completion of the first round of Periodic Reporting, a world-wide survey of the state of World Heritage sites implemented through the UNESCO World Heritage Centre 1999–2005. Not unexpectedly, this has revealed the state of World Heritage on the ground to be, in general, often poor, even parlous and characteristically under threat. The World Heritage Committee is now thinking that its prime concern should perhaps be the proper conservation of the sites it has already identified as 'of universal value' by inscribing them on the World Heritage List, rather the annual, somewhat undignified and now highly politicised scrabble to inscribe another several dozen sites on the List. Yet, such sensible, realistic constraint is politically impossible given the globally unbalanced distribution of World Heritage sites – the great majority are in developed countries – and the active implementation of a highly proper policy to adjust the imbalance, at least geographically if not proportionately, by encouraging nominations from countries with few or no inscriptions.

It is in this context that it was and is hoped that 'cultural landscapes' can be particularly helpful in World Heritage terms, since they offer a means of recognising internationally a range of heritages that are non-monumental. While such can occur anywhere, cultural achievement expressed in landscapes, wood, mud, stories and art can be 'of universal value' just as much as those stone buildings and architectural *ensembles* which so characterise the Euro-centric World Heritage List (WHC 2003a). Unfortunately, however, these so often occur in those parts of the world which are economically under-resourced, with perhaps little or no capacity for the big professional and bureaucratic effort now required to make a nomination and subsequently – as the Periodic Reporting exercises have exposed – to sustain the management effort necessary to conserve those significant values which brought World Heritage status in the first place.

CHARACTERISTICS OF WORLD HERITAGE CULTURAL LANDSCAPES

Already by 2001 World Heritage cultural landscapes were defining themselves in terms of characteristics which seemed to be significant in their nature and management (Fowler 2003a, 30–34). Certain characteristics were recurring in different landscapes and, while no one cultural landscape possessed the whole suite, most shared several common characteristics. Now, with a 'population' of 53 World Heritage cultural landscapes (WHCLs) to examine, we can see that nearly all exhibit six to nine characteristics from a common list of 13 such descriptors (Fowler 2003a & b, 2004, 182–86, Table 9).

These characteristics are:

A = significant aesthetic quality
B = buildings, often large buildings
C = continuity of lifeway/landuse is an important element
F = farming/agriculture is/was a major element in the nature of the landscape
G = ornamental garden(s)/park(s)
I = primarily an industrial Site
L = the landscape is, or contains elements which are, significant for group identity
M = a mountain is, or mountains are, an integral part of the landscape
P = a locally-resident population is significant
R = the landscape possesses an important dimension of religiosity/sanctity/holiness
S = survival is a significant theme in the landscape, physically as of such as ancient field systems, and/or socially, as of a group of people in a hostile environment
T = towns, and/or villages
W = water is an integral, or at least significant, part of the landscape

Using these characteristics and other, factual data, an attempt was made to analyse the 36 WHCLs up to and including 2003 (Fowler 2004, Table 9). Those data are summarised below (Table 1, row 1, using as headings the letters to designate the characteristics as listed above), compared with the similarly summarised data from 2004–05 (row 2), and consolidated into a summary for the whole period during which it has been possible to inscribe cultural landscapes on the World Heritage list (Table 1, row 3):

The list of 13 characteristics was internally generated by the 53 WHCLs themselves. I did not invent them; I merely jotted down what appeared to be

Table 1   World Heritage Cultural Landscapes 2004–05: a Character Analysis.

Row	Years	No. of WHCLs	A	B	C	F	G	I	L	M	P	R	S	T	W
1	1993–2003	37	21	24	24	20	11	2	21	17	16	15	15	24	21
2	2004–2005	16	7	10	13	9	2	1	9	6	10	6	11	10	7
3	1993–2005	53	28	34	37	29	13	3	30	23	26	21	26	34	28
4	*Ranking of characteristics*	53	**6=**	**2=**	**1**	**5**	**12**	**13**	**4**	**10**	**8=**	**11**	**8=**	**2=**	**6=**

salient characteristics of each WHCL individually and noted that some of them, not altogether surprisingly, kept recurring. Table 1, row 4, shows a ranking of the characteristics based on the frequency of their occurrence among the 53 World Heritage cultural landscapes. Thus characteristic C, 'continuity', appears more often than any other characteristic, 37 times among 53 WHCLs; characteristic B, 'buildings', often large ones, and T, 'towns and/or villages', occur almost as often. This is telling us that WHCLs are characteristically not wilderness or deserted areas, as with so many landscapes of nature conservation, but well-established, long-occupied places (Rössler 2004). In contrast, industrial landscapes (column I) are barely represented among the 53 WHCLs, underlining a well-known WH Committee prejudice; though ornamental gardens/parks, the second least popular type of WHCL (column G), makes up or is a significant part of 13 of the 53.

The recognition of this unconsciously-created 'character' phenomenon of WHCLs is important for management: maybe there are a number of precepts which can be recommended for the genre of World Heritage cultural landscape. In particular, it surely suggests that management in many cases should include, or actually be based on, concepts and techniques from the worlds of urban conservation and Town and Country Planning rather than be taken without question from Nature conservation alone. My own belief is that, learning of course from landscape management for other purposes, we nevertheless need to develop a philosophy and a suite of practices specific to the management of World Heritage cultural landscapes: they are, after all, by definition sui generis, with unique objectives, and not merely protected wildlife habitats (as defined, for example, in IUCN 1994), National Parks or urban conservation areas by any other name.

As important as the shared character of WHCLs, is the diversity represented by the numbers in Table 1. Mountains (M) and sanctity (R) may be among the lower-counting numbers, for example, but the strength of the WHCL concept lies in the fact that any one of those can combine with any one or more of the other main characteristics – and indeed other characteristics beyond – to create a landscape unique not only to the eye but to the mind. So, while analysis of the full and growing portfolio WHCLs characterizes the genre as full of diversity and variety in one plane (WHC 2003a), in another we see a tendency towards homogeneity. This is not an outcome envisaged in 1992, or even 2000.

NOTES ON SOME LANDSCAPES, 2004–07

My observations here are based on a number of actual or potential World Heritage sites with which I happen to have been involved, and in most cases have visited, between May 2004 and February 2006. This empirical collection of sites and landscapes provides considerable variety of both location and type of site/landscape. It should also illustrate a diversity of issues, political and managerial; but while at one level the places indeed demonstrate a diversity of issues, at another level experience can lead to the recognition on a new site of one or more of fundamentally the same ten or so management challenges. Such challenges centre on politics, resources, management structure, personnel, residents, conservation, access, tourism, education and threats. I can only touch on some of those here in picking out at most two points from each site selected.

I resist the temptation of another fling on **Hadrian's Wall** (inscribed **1987**) where the creation of a National Trail along and within a World Heritage site continues to raise interesting management issues (Austen and Young 2005, Fowler 2005a & b). I also limit myself to but one point current at Avebury (see Pomeroy-Kellinger, this volume). Partly arising from the revised management Plan (English Heritage 2005), partly from recent decisions about Stonehenge (see Bedu this volume), discussion is currently in train about the use of the phrase 'cultural landscape' to describe the World Heritage site. Officialdom in England does not like the use of the phrase at all in respect of Avebury, despite the fact that the Avebury landscape is a cultural landscape and that it is perfectly proper for people to describe it as such. It, with Stonehenge, is included in the list of 70 World Heritage sites which are, or contain, cultural landscapes (Fowler 2003a, Annex C, 103), as distinct from the official list of 53 World Heritage cultural landscapes. In the light of the Inspector's (incorrect) judgement at the Stonehenge 'Roads' Inquiry that the World Heritage Site there was about the monuments and not the spaces between them, some are worried that a retro-trend might be emerging in official thinking about these matters. The trend is moving away from the holistic concept of historic landscape or historic environment in favour of the archaic (but bureaucratically easier) notion that heritage, in this case World Heritage, consists of specific monuments, archaeological sites, not the whole context in which such sites exist.

As far as the World Heritage Convention (UNESCO 1972) and the *Operational Guidelines* (UNESCO 2005) are concerned, the whole of the area within the boundary agreed at the inscription of a World Heritage site is the World Heritage site. The concept does not allow of hierarchy within the site: it is all of equal 'universal value'. There are not 'important' and 'not so important' bits within a World Heritage site. Avebury henge monument is not of higher World Heritage merit than the village and farmed fields among which it sits: it is precisely the whole and the relationships it contains and expresses which give the place its 'universal value'.

Another village is also on my list (Fowler 2003a, Annex C, 103) within the breath-taking archipelago of **St Kilda** (**1986, 2004, 2005**) (Fig.1) on the edge of western Europe, 64 km west of the Outer Hebrides. Having, in World Heritage terms, been successively inscribed as a natural site and then a marine site, it is now officially a cultural landscape (**2005**; it possesses nine of the characteristics listed above). The only aspect on which I comment here is the intellectual one – not always a dimension to the fore in nominating World Heritage sites. The challenge came after a referral from the World Heritage Committee

in 2004 of a re-nomination to extend the World Heritage status to the marine environment in which the islands sit and to the cultural landscape dimension of their surfaces (NTS 2003). The former was accepted, the latter was not, with a polite request for a more comprehensive comparative study of similar places.

The challenge was, then, to research analogues of St Kilda in World Heritage terms, though not necessarily limited to World Heritage sites, and in effect to conceptualise and re-present the archipelago in such a way that outsiders clearly could understand its claims to be a cultural landscape and one of 'outstanding universal value'. The global comparative exercise was crucial, for the original nomination was bedded in the supposed exceptional place of St Kilda in regional archaeology and history, a short landscape chronology, and the halo effect of an iconic abandonment of the island by its remaining inhabitants in 1930. Such failed to convince in World Heritage terms. A great deal of academic research and re-thinking, however, resulted in a different representation successfully re-submitted in 2005. The correctness of that decision was re-inforced by the independent publication of Andrew Flemming's

Figure 1   St Kilda: view eastwards from high above the west end of Village Bay, Hirta.
Showing some of the detail of part of the multi-phase cultural landscape, notably the village street abandoned 1930 and now modestly conserved, the enclosed circular cemetery, the boundary wall, the elongated parcels of land to north up the mountain flanks and south towards the sea and, dotted around in a non-random pattern, many cleits, essentially turf-roofed, drystone-walled sheds for drying and storage (cf Fleming 2005).

(2005) brilliant book about St. Kilda, though he had of course already made his material and thoughts available to the National Trust for Scotland. Academic research fed straight into status and into better management through better understanding.

LATIN AMERICA

Visits to two countries in South America, Peru and Argentina, raised two deep issues which arise in many parts of the world when we try to manage our cultural inheritance. The Andes along the eastern side of Peru are littered with archaeological sites and historic landscapes; they are also home to indigenous peoples, often farming traditional crops in traditional ways largely, sometimes exclusively, based on manual labour alleviated only by the donkey for porterage and some modest traction. A common sight is what appears to be half a haystack wobbling along the side a track: beneath it is a donkey or human taking food back home. These people are very poor financially; their mountainous environment is difficult and often hostile; yet, in living as best they can in these circumstances, they have made and are sustaining visually striking landscapes of considerable scientific interest. But of course it is the conjunction of the 'hardware' represented by the landscapes and structures with the 'software' of the lifeway and its traditional toolkit of implements and practices which creates the 'magic' of such places in outsiders' eyes and minds. There are many other such places in South America, some of them discussed in cultural landscape and World Heritage terms in Barreda's pioneering survey (2002). They raise questions beyond management: not just how to manage them in heritage and conservation terms but also how to choose those for such treatment and, more profoundly, whether such conservation intervention is justifiable anyway. What, after all, is the interested country doing when it designates such an area for conservation management? – asking the residents to continue to be poor, to continue working the land without machines and electricity? And at the same time to view with stoicism the intrusion of visitors, professionals and tourists, into their lives and homes?

Further south along the Andes I found myself in precisely this situation in real life at the World Heritage site of **Quebrada de Humahuaca (2003)** in the extreme north west of Argentina, close to the Bolivian border (Neilson 2004, Perkins 2002). It lies in Jujuy, the poorest province in the country. I was there to participate in a Workshop intended to identify the 'Lineaments for a Management Plan for the Quebrada de Humahuaca World Heritage Site ...' (Fowler 2006a). The site had been inscribed on the List by the World Heritage Committee, inexplicably and most unwisely, without a management plan, and management there had subsequently run into one or two local difficulties. Our role was to advise on developing an appropriate management plan but it was very

quickly obvious that at stake was far more than the absence of a plan (Fowler 2006b).

The Quebrada itself, some 10–15,000 ft (3000–4500 m) above sea level, is a gorge through treeless, mountainous country with colourful exposed geology, an obviously dynamic geomorphology, a water problem, a major highway and a defunct 20th century railway line. A few thousand residents live in a string of villages/small towns, characteristically with 'historic cores' of Spanish-colonial aspect in their plans and architecture, along a Rio Grande which can vary between a trickle and a torrent. The traditional lifeway centres on ovid pastoralism. The cacti are magnificent: 6 metres high, they watch your every step like irregular ranks of android sentries.

Real sentries stop traffic on the historic highway through the gorge, for it is the main route between the Pacific and Atlantic Oceans, from Chile and Bolivia to Argentina and the port of Buenos Aires. The gorge and a large area of uninhabited mountainscape to either side is on the World Heritage List primarily – but mistakenly in my view – because of this 'cultural route', part of the former the Carmino Inca, within it. This route is itself currently being considered as a potential World Heritage cultural itinerary along its whole length but the abundant archaeology in the landscape, somewhat unappreciated in the nomination and by management so far, suggests a long-term pre-Inca settlement of the area in a nature/people relationship troubled but workable on its own terms rather than merely hanging on to the coat-tails of passing trade (Fig. 2).

So there has been and is a basic difference in perspective of the place (and not only locally: ICOMOS recommended inscription, without a completed management plan, as 'a cultural route'). This is not a good thing on which to base successful management in the first place. And then there are the people: I have not previously come across such a strong and common sense of grievance in a heritage context. Whatever the rights and wrongs of the situation, many residents of the Quebrada, notably the indigenous people, blame the act of inscription of the Quebrada onto the World Heritage List in July 2003 as the reason for their manifest current ills.

The pertinent value here is criterion (v): it was inscribed because it is 'an outstanding example of a traditional human settlement [and] land use which is representative of a culture (or cultures), especially when it has become vulnerable under the impact of irreversible change'. But in this case it might well be that putting the Quebrada on the World Heritage List both to acknowledge its outstanding nature and help conserve it contributes to the opposite effect. Without political will to tackle the situation, and without a planning control system in place, this World Heritage site could easily lose within a decade those values for which it was inscribed. Yet, on a continent sorely underrepresented on its List, World Heritage simply cannot allow, nor can its reputation

Figure 2   Coctaca, part of the Quebrada de Humahuaca World Heritage site, Argentina.
East of the main gorge, this photograph shows an extensive and remarkable area of dry-stone walls defining small enclosures, supposedly 'agricultural structures', that is plots/small fields, and, more specifically, 'state fields' of the conquering Inca in the 15th century AD, although it is probable that the systems originated in pre-Inca times. The site appears in publicity as one of the outstanding places of the area yet it enjoys no visitor facilities, conservation management or on-site interpretation.

afford to allow, a magnificent cultural landscape of genuinely 'outstanding universal value' to slide into a denial of those very values for which it has been brought to world attention.

THE CARIBBEAN

Similar factors, not least poverty and politics, can quickly demand attention when looking thematically at a whole region or at the heritage potential of a single country; hence the several useful regional studies of cultural landscapes e.g. Barreda 2002, Rössler and Saouma-Forero 2000, and the purpose of Tentative Lists (UNESCO 2005, paras. 62–76). The Caribbean region is one identified by the World Heritage Committee as particularly deserving of encouragement in bringing forward World Heritage nominations; it is thought that landscapes may offer one way of meeting this objective in a region where cultural properties already on the List are dominated by colonial structures, often militaristic (Fowler 2005c). A regional problem, however, is that, on the one hand, 'heritage' tends to be seen in such colonial, non-indigenous terms while, on the other,

a largely intangible 'indigenous' heritage ranges from pre-European cultures of a non-structural character to a style of popular music blossoming in the second half of the 20th century around a cult of Bob Marley.

An acceptable vehicle for advancing World Heritage in the Caribbean appears to be the plantation and its landscape: introduced admittedly, but places showing great variety island to island depending upon environment, crop(s) and colonial power. Furthermore, these are the places where the forebears of many of the islands' present-day populations lived and worked, indeed the reason why these ancestors were brought to the Caribbean in the first place. So, unlike classic European military fortifications, plantations possess a strong Afro-Caribbean dimension which, now that the former slave plantations are history, resonate with many among the insular inhabitants today.

Two World Heritage cultural landscapes exist in the Caribbean already, both on Cuba: the working **Viñales Valley (1999;** Brief Descriptions 2003, 16) and the abandoned **Archaeological Landscape of the First Coffee Plantations in the South-East**

of Cuba (2000). Any archaeological landscape at the latter is buried under sub-tropical vegetation and inaccessible except immediately around the plantation house. Here, the buildings clearly represent a major conservation problem, hemmed in as they are by pressing rain-forest. 'Unique' though the site may be, the management issues surrounding it were all too familiar, while its qualities of 'outstanding universal value' are certainly well-hidden.

Politics, local, inter-island and regional, were in mind in drafting the 'Santiago de Cuba Declaration on Cultural Landscapes in the Caribbean' which came out of a UNESCO meeting in November 2005. I quote the first part of the draft *in extenso* because, for both the Caribbean and elsewhere, it so well exemplifies many issues, including those touched on in the section on Latin America above. The Declaration stated that:

– *cultural landscapes are well represented in the Caribbean and are probably the most complete tangible expression of the heritage in the sub-region ...*
– *Caribbean cultural landscapes, in addition to their significance as examples of the historical relationship between human beings and their natural environment, offer an enormous potential for the sustainable development and given their immense capacity for certain productions, cultural tourism, leisure and recreation;*
– *a large part of the landscapes in the Caribbean are not yet duly identified, documented or acknowledged as heritage sites in their territories and countries or by their inhabitants;*
– *cultural landscapes are generally complex entities that may extend over a large territory on land or sea, belong to several jurisdictions, contain various forms of heritage and concern various actors, all this contributing to give a greater complexity to the accurate definition of their boundary and setting, and their management which, with few exceptions, needs to be reinforced;*
several challenges exist arising from the need to address jointly the conservation goals for cultural landscapes in the Caribbean while improving living conditions for local populations or facing social changes;
the threats to Caribbean cultural landscapes are many and growing, often amplified by the lack of human and financial resources or tools such as Risk Preparedness Plans. These threats include frequent and destructive natural disasters, the adverse effects of weathering and other physical factors to the characteristics of most of the small island Caribbean States, the impact of mass tourism, arbitrary urban or industrial expansion, the negative impacts of globalisation and the presence of local or foreign actors working against the integrity and authenticity of the site's values. Additionally, some traditional techniques and crafts are in danger of disappearing.'

The Declaration went on to make numerous recommendations to all Caribbean States Party to the Convention of 1972, including the setting up of programmes and projects to identify, document and inventory the cultural landscapes, and the establishment of guidelines for the comprehensive management of cultural landscapes. Overall, take away the specific Caribbean elements and the Declaration becomes a model for desiderata, policies and a programme of action for landscape conservation anywhere, though many issues behind this Declaration are politically sensitive, for it is addressed to numerous constitutionally distinct island entities.

PALESTINE

One legal entity, which, as per the Cuba Declaration above, has taken on board advice 'to identify, document and inventory' its heritage in World Heritage terms, is not yet able to nominate to the List. Palestine is not a State and therefore not able to become a signatory to the Convention, but it aspires to be both. (My two visits were in 2004, so my reportage and impressions relate to the situation before the election and change of government early in 2006.) That it should be thinking about and preparing for nominating its first World Heritage sites in present circumstances may seem remarkable in, even peripheral to, the politically highly-charged situation in which it finds itself; but the Palestinian National Authority, numerous other bodies and enough individuals to matter are well aware of the existence and potential importance of the 'heritage' in the West Bank and Gaza. The main reasons for this, in order of importance, are clear: religious, religious and religious; political, not least in terms of national pride and the identity of what one day will be a new, autonomous Palestinian state; economic, in terms of the potential contribution a tourist industry can make to a poor, new state; and finally scientific.

In 2002, the world was shocked to see on its TV screens a prolonged siege of the Church of the Nativity, Bethlehem; the Church was in fact damaged. So too was the historic core of the 'Biblical' city of Nablus. These episodes triggered outside concern not just for that Church but for other sites in the Holy Land; the World Heritage Committee expressed its particular and immediate concern; and it set aside resources for an assessment of the state of the heritage in Palestine including the identification of possible future World Heritage sites which might be considered in different political circumstances. Hence an upsurge of local effort and interest and the arrival under UNESCO auspices of various forms of outside assistance.

My own brief was to contribute a World Heritage perspective to the 30 plus sites and areas initially identified as possibilities by knowledgeable local people; which meant visiting them, if possible with the local experts. Over the two visits, we managed to reach most, despite one or two nervous incidents. The result is an Inventory of Cultural and Natural Heritage Sites of Potential Outstanding Universal Value in Palestine, published in June 2005 (PNA 2005). This was in time for the World Heritage Committee's meeting in Durban, just three years after it expressed its initial concern. Things do not always move with such rapidity in UNESCO-land.

The Inventory identifies and documents 20 sites in what is in effect a provisional Tentative List. Each site is judged in the light of the World Heritage criteria which could well be used come the time for a formal nomination, with a statement of its outstanding universal value, integrity and authenticity in the context of a brief comparison with relevant places. It is important that this first list does not have the effect of ossifying Palestine's and the world's concept of Palestinian heritage. Nevertheless, there is more than enough to be going on with: after Bethlehem and Tell es-Sultan (Fig. 3) come Hebron Old Town, Mount Gerizim and the Samaritans, and Qumran; the Dead Sea is seventh, Nablus Old Town

is twelfth, and as far down the list as sixteenth is Sebastia, ancient Samaria in a landscape associated with John the Baptist.

Our consideration widened from a single monument-based approach to include two other types of potential World Heritage sites, heritage themes and cultural landscapes. Looking, for example, at the Umayyad site called Hisham's Palace near Jericho – not in itself a potential World Heritage site – we wondered about the feasibility of a potential transfrontier nomination around the theme of 'Umayyad palaces' in which it might be included with related sites in Lebanon, Jordan and Syria.

We also noted two possible cultural landscapes, one a particular place with a very specific character and associations, the other more an idea for which the appropriate landscapes have still to be researched. El-Bariyah is the place, the 'wilderness' of Jesus' 'forty days and forty nights' and still a 'mountainous desert habitat ... essentially a treeless, thinsoiled, arid and dramatically eroded limestone plateau ... dissected by wadi draining towards the

Figure 3   Tell es-Sultan, Palestine, better-known archaeologically simply as 'Jericho', is a large tell at the core of 'Old' or 'Ancient' Jericho as distinct from the larger modern town to the east.
Here as viewed from the far too adjacent visitor car-park on its south are glimpses of prehistoric walls, exposed but embedded in the tell's stratigraphy, of the serious erosion from which the archaeological layers and structures suffer, and of the visitor path (top right). But the real point of the photograph is of course to show the cable cars gliding not very far above the World Heritage Site. Their function is religious pilgrimage, not cultural tourism; but whatever their motivation, they represent a physical, visual and audio intrusion unacceptable by normal World Heritage management standards.

Figure 4   Mar Saba, Palestine, is an isolated, living monastery founded in the 5th century AD in El-Bariyah, the desert east of Bethlehem, where Jesus fasted and Bedouin still tend their flocks of goats.
This environmentally-hostile place, once vegetated but long over stressed by aridity and grazing, of considerable natural interest and almost overloaded with cultural values, is now identified as a possible World Heritage cultural landscape.

Dead Sea' (PNA 2005, 23). Inhabited long before the first century AD, it was subsequently colonised by Christian hermits. Some of their places of refuge developed into monasteries: 73 existed either side of AD 500, among them Mar Saba, built c 450, still in use and clinging dramatically to the cliffs of the Kidron valley (Fig. 4). Later Islamic holy sites remain important places on the Muslim pilgrimage route to Mecca.

The idea of finding one or more areas of appropriate 'cultural landscape' arose from the common description of Palestine as the 'Land of olives and vines' (PNA 2005, 28). Now that land is becoming more and more heavily used and broken up by military and political demands in addition to pressures for economic development, it has already become difficult to identify characteristic areas of olive and vine cultivation large enough to meet World Heritage desiderata and containing in good order a suite of characteristic landscape features – for example, terraces, tracks, watch-towers and field storage buildings – and traditional working practices and implements. Nevertheless, landscapes of the olive and the vine, certainly not unique to Palestine but so

redolent in their symbolism and Biblical imagery of the Holy Land, are included in the Inventory not only because it is a good idea expressing 'outstanding universal value' but also because 'there is an urgent need to protect olive trees and vineyard terracing, and all their associated structures and landscape features, to assure their future as an authentic cultural heritage component of the Palestinian landscape' (PNA 2005, 29).

DISCUSSION

My fortuitous forays into current World Heritage illustrate a wide, and perhaps worrying, range of issues, notably management issues. Matters of area, space, definition – territorial issues – commonly reappear, as do ones concerning the people living in the area inscribed, whether they be indigenous or incoming. Interfaces with other designations are not always happy: an area and organisation appropriate to a National Park, for example, are not necessarily appropriate to a World Heritage site, especially where it is a cultural landscape. Sacred places and associations frequently are, or occur in, World

Figure 5 Ginkaku-ji temple garden, Kyoto, Japan.
With at least seven of the characteristics listed on p. 65, exemplifies in its fragility, beauty and tranquillity sensitive management of a cultural landscape in a World Heritage site stemming from belief and ritual requirements without 'benefit' of a Western-style management plan.

Heritage sites and are indeed often the reason, or a main reason, for it enjoying such status; but religion itself, and particularly conflicting religions, can become a major management issue.

A central management issue is whether a management plan really is a requirement for World Heritage purposes. In my view, it is, partly because I know too many sites where the lack of such a written plan leads to trouble and partly because, even if a site is being well managed by traditional practices, for example in controlling grazing regimes in Africa or in maintaining a delicate temple garden in Kyoto (Fig. 5), it can only help to write down what is being done and why even if the main function of doing so is to help outsiders understand what is going on. But above all, in my experience, it is the joint creation of such a plan over months and probably several years, rather than the plan itself, which is of incalculable value in developing a successful management regime. For that reason, while outsiders can help, I do not believe that the parachuting in experts,

who afterwards disappear, to write a management plan in a short time is the best way forward. Furthermore, a World Heritage management plan does not have to be formulated in rigid Western mode. Nevertheless, something needs to be written down to identify the particular 'outstanding universal value' in each case so that all know what is to be maintained.

The identification and appropriate management of landscapes are one of the main ways forward for World Heritage. It is land, their land, which speaks most directly to many of the remaining (c 50%) rural population of the world; and many living in cities and town look out to their roots in local, rural landscapes. Nevertheless, urban, industrial and thematic landscapes, together with routes of various sorts, should also be developed as World Heritage sites and as cultural landscapes in particular. All should be managed primarily as World Heritage Sites yet it is unfortunately clear that, with a small number of exceptions, we have not yet learned how to do that. This is principally because the precepts of World Heritage as expressed in the *Guidelines* (UNESCO 2005), especially that of exemplarity, have not been accepted as priority. We are still fitting 'World Heritage' around and into existing concepts and provision, including the national designation and local plan. Such conventional thinking may well hinder the intellectual and practical development of new sorts of cultural landscape built up around urban and industrial areas, around themes such as emigration/immigration and basic foodstuffs such as yams and tea, and along routes of, for example, exploration, trade, military campaigns and great leaders and artists. Whatever their context, new sites as well as most existing ones demand that we ask ourselves from first principles what is required of us in the 21st century to manage a World Heritage site as such.

At the 30-year commemorative World Heritage Conference in Venice in 2002, Nicola Bono, Under-Secretary for Culture, welcoming delegates to Italy, spoke of 'a pledge of undivided commitment to ensuring that heritage is preserved intact for future generations, both in physical terms and in terms of the values linked to its traditional use and the identity-related importance attributed to it by the local populations' (WHC 2003b, 22). In other words, though I do not think anyone actually said this: 'World Heritage is about people.'

It was the artist Paul Nash (1938) who did say, long before World Heritage landscapes and the need to manage them were conceptualised:

All these things under consideration here – stones, bones, empty fields, demolished houses, and back gardens – all these have their trivial features, as it were their blind side; but, also, they have another character, and this is neither moral nor sentimental nor literary, but rather something strange and – for want of a better word, which may not exist – poetical.

Figure 6   The Avebury landscape, Wiltshire, has motivated antiquarians and scholars and inspired poets, writers and artists, here exemplified by the author's 'Avebury landscape 2', 2004.
In the mid-20th century Paul Nash explored megaliths, mystery and metaphor here in great paintings and, while management inevitably concerns itself with the pragmatic and prosaic, the 'other' in this landscape continues to stimulate artistic attempts to capture the 'poetical'.

Words which could well be the caption to Figure 6. Managing poetry in the landscape, is that the challenge? Think about it.

BIBLIOGRAPHY

Austen, P, and Young, C, 2005 Finding the way, *British Archaeology* **83**, (July/August 2005), 43–45

Barreda, E M, (ed.) 2002 *Paisajes Culturales en los Andes*, Paris: World Heritage Centre, UNESCO

Brief Descriptions 2003 = *Brief Descriptions of the 754 properties inscribed on the World Heritage List 2003*, Paris: UNESCO (up-to-date version available on the Internet @ *http://whc.unesco.org/brief.htm*)

English Heritage, 2005 *Avebury World Heritage Site Management Plan*, London:

Fleming, A, 2005 *St Kilda and the Wider World. Tales of an Iconic Island*, Macclesfield, UK: Windgather Press

Fowler, P, 2003a *World Heritage Cultural Landscapes 1992–2002*, Paris: UNESCO, World Heritage Papers 6

Fowler, P, 2003b World Heritage cultural landscapes 1992–2002: a review and prospect, in WHC 2003a, 16–32

Fowler, P, 2004 *Landscapes for the World: conserving a global heritage*, Macclesfield, UK: Windgather Press

Fowler, P, 2005a *Hadrian's Wall and the National Trail: a note on a visit, 18–19 July 2005*, London: privately published and distributed

Fowler, P, 2005b Trail on Trial, *Hadrian's Wall News* **27** (December 2005), 10–11

Fowler, P, 2005c Cultural landscapes in the world, a paper given at a UNESCO meeting on 'Cultural landscapes in the Caribbean: identification and safeguarding strategies', Santiago de Cuba, 7–10 November, 2005 (publication forthcoming)

Fowler P, 2006a Conceptualizing management of the Quebrada de Humahuaca. Analytical approaches towards a management plan for an Andean cultural landscape on the World Heritage List, London: Paper 1 on Quebrada de Humahuaca for the World Heritage Centre under UNESCO Contract 500027545

Fowler P, 2006b Towards an appropriate management plan for the Quebrada de Humahuaca World Heritage site, Argentina. A landscape approach to an Andean World Heritage cultural landscape, London: Paper 2 on Quebrada de Humahuaca for the World Heritage Centre under UNESCO Contract 500027545

UNESCO 1972 *Convention Concerning the Protection of the World Cultural and Natural Heritage.*
Website: http://whc.unesco.org/en/convention text/

UNESCO 2005 *Operational Guidelines for the Implementation of the World Heritage Convention*, Paris: UNESCO, World Heritage Centre, WHC.05/2 (2 February 2005)

IUCN 1994 *Guidelines for Protected Area Management Categories*, Gland, Switzerland and Cambridge, UK: IUCN

Mujica, E J, 2003 Cultural landscapes and the challenges of conservation in Latin America and the Caribbean, in WHC 2003a, 82–88

Nash 1938 Paul Nash, *Country Life*, 21 May 1938, quoted in Montague J. 2003, *Paul Nash. Modern Artist, Ancient Landscape*, London: Tate Publishing, 66

Neilson, A E, 2004 *Quebrada de Humahuaca, Provincia de Jujuy, Argentina. A Cultural Itinerary with 10,000 Years of History*, Jujuy, Argentina: Gobierno de Jujuy

NTS 2003 *Revised Nomination of St Kilda for inclusion in the World Heritage Site List*, Edinburgh: National Trust for Scotland

Perkins, C, (ed.) 2002 *The Treasures of the Quebrada de Humahuaca*, Tilcarra, Argentina: Thomas Gibson Fine Art Ltd

PNA 2005 Palestinian National Authority 2005 *Inventory of Cultural and Natural Heritage Sites of Potential Outstanding Universal Value in Palestine*, Ramallah, Palestine: Department of Antiquities and Cultural Heritage, Ministry of Tourism and Antiquities

Rössler, M, 2003 Linking Nature and Culture: World Heritage Cultural Landscapes, in WHC 2003a, 10–15

Rössler, M, and Saouma-Forero, G, (eds) 2000 *The World Heritage Convention and Cultural Landscapes in Africa*, Paris: UNESCO

WHC 2003a *Cultural Landscapes: the challenges of conservation*, Paris: UNESCO, World Heritage Papers 7

WHC 2003b *World Heritage 2002. Shared Legacy, Common Responsibility*, Paris: UNESCO, World Heritage Centre